590 599
Ear
       Earnest, Don
Life in Zoos & Preserves

Wild, Wild World of Animals

(Time-Life Television)

MARA NP

GAYLORD M

Wild, Wild World of Animals

Life in Zoos &
Preserves

A TIME-LIFE TELEVISION BOOK

Editor: Charles Osborne
Associate Editors: Bonnie Johnson, Joan Chambers
   Author: Don Earnest
   Writers: Deborah Heineman, Cecilia Waters
   Literary Research: Ellen Schachter
   Text Research: Maureen Duffy Benziger, Melissa Wanamaker
Picture Editor: Judith Greene
   Permissions and Production: Cecilia Waters
Designer: Constance A. Timm
   Art Assistant: Carl Van Brunt
Copy Editor: Eleanor Van Bellingham
   Copy Staff: Robert Braine, Florence Tarlow

WILD, WILD WORLD OF ANIMALS
TELEVISION PROGRAM
Producers: Jonathan Donald and Lothar Wolff
This Time-Life Television Book is published by Time-Life Films, Inc.
Bruce L. Paisner, *President*
J. Nicoll Durrie, *Vice President*

THE AUTHOR

DON EARNEST was formerly a staff writer and editor with Time-Life Books. He has contributed to two previous volumes in this series, *Insects & Spiders* and *Birds of Field & Forest*, is the co-author of *Life in the Coral Reef* and the author of *Songbirds*.

THE CONSULTANTS

MARY K. EVENSEN received an M.S. in zoology from the University of Minnesota. She is currently working toward her Ph.D. in biology at Queens College of The City University of New York.

SIDNEY HORENSTEIN is on the staff of the Department of Invertebrates at the American Museum of Natural History, New York, and the Department of Geology and Geography, Hunter College. He has written many articles on natural history and has been a consultant on numerous Time-Life books. He publishes *New York City Notes on Natural History* and is Associate Editor of *Fossils Magazine*.

JOHN FARRAND JR. is a member of the staff of the Department of Ornithology at the American Museum of Natural History in New York. He is the co-author of *The Audubon Society Guides to North American Birds: Eastern Region*.

THE COVER: The lesser panda is a herbivorous Asiatic relative of the omnivorous raccoon. The size of a large house cat, the panda lives among rocks and trees in the Himalayas.

Wild, Wild World of Animals

Life in Zoos & Preserves

Based on the television series
Wild, Wild World of Animals

Published by
TIME-LIFE FILMS

The excerpt from Menagerie Manor by Gerald Durrell, copyright © 1964 by Gerald
Durrell, is reprinted by permission of Viking Press Inc. and Curtis Brown, Ltd.

The excerpt from "Why the Bear Waddles When He Walks," from American
Indian Mythologies, by Alice Marriott and Carol K. Rachlin, copyright © 1968,
originally published by Thomas Y. Crowell, is reprinted by permission of Harper
& Row Publishers, Inc. and Marie Rodell—Frances Collin Agency.

The excerpt from Idle Days in Patagonia by W.H. Hudson is reprinted courtesy of
E.P. Dutton & Co., Inc. and Agents Society of Authors, London.

The excerpt from The Lost World of the Kalahari by Laurens van der Post,
copyright © 1958 by Laurens van der Post, is reprinted by permission of William
Morrow and Company, Inc. and The Hogarth Press.

ISBN 0-913948-21-7

Library of Congress Catalog Card Number: 78-56897

Printed in the United States of America.

Contents

INTRODUCTION 8
by Don Earnest

ZOOS 16
A selection from Menagerie Manor
by Gerald Durrell . . . 24

AMERICAN GRASSLANDS 40
Why the Bear Waddles When He Walks
A Comanche Tale . . . 56

PATAGONIA 62
A selection from Idle Days in Patagonia
by W. H. Hudson . . . 66

CAMARGUE AND COTO DONAÑA 76

SOUTHERN AFRICA 92
A selection from The Lost World of the Kalahari
by Laurens van der Post . . . 100

THE INDIAN SUBCONTINENT 108

CREDITS AND BIBLIOGRAPHY 126

INDEX 127

Introduction
by Don Earnest

Patrick, the first Indian rhinoceros born live in the Western Hemisphere, at the age of four months poses in his stall at the National Zoo in Washington, D.C. Born in January 1974, Patrick is on loan to New York's Bronx Zoo for breeding purposes.

LESS THAN 500 YEARS AGO, when Columbus's trio of tiny ships landed at San Salvador, the newfound Americas were untouched lands blessed with an extraordinarily bountiful wildlife. But they were far from unique. Australia was undiscovered, the interior of Africa south of the Sahara was unexplored, and even Europe, which had borne the brunt of man's development over centuries, still had large regions that were blanketed with dense, game-filled forests. Around 1750, during the industrial revolution, the population of the entire world was still small, totaling less than the present census for Europe alone. It has been in the brief span of only a little over two centuries that man's mushrooming numbers and increasing technological capabilities have radically altered the face of the earth and reduced hundreds of species of wild creatures to their present threatened or endangered condition.

Recognition of this condition—and of its implications for the survival of man himself—is an even more recent phenomenon. The concept of setting aside areas in the wilderness for the protection of animals from man is the fruit of the last century. So is the modern zoo, an environment especially designed and built for the preservation of animals as well as for their display. In the years since World War II, the zoo concept has been refined toward emphasis on scientific education and the breeding of wild animals in captivity. This book offers a look at a representative sampling of some 526 major zoos and 698 preserves, or national parks, and reserves around the world. (Reserves generally denote areas where animals share their environment to some extent with the local human population.)

The recent movement toward the protection of animals is a belated acknowledgment that in pushing any species over the brink of extinction, man risks rending the ecological fabric connecting the human species to other creatures and that the consequences of such unraveling cannot be foreseen. Wildlife expert Bernhard Grzimek says, "We must realize that we are animals too—we eat the same food and breathe the same air and live from the same soil." He believes that "Every species dying out is a warning of the death of mankind," and his views claim more and more adherents.

Though many individual species of animals have been brought to the verge of extinction by hunting and other forms of killing, more overall harm to wildlife has demonstrably resulted from human alterations of the environment carried through with no thought for wild animals at all. It was the clearing of the great woods that covered nearly all of the eastern third of North America and much of central Europe that brought about the precipitous decline in those continents' wildlife populations. In more recent times the cutting of tropical forests for agriculture has endangered the gorilla in Africa, the rare aye-aye lemur in Madagascar, the spider monkey in Costa Rica and a host of other creatures that depend on the dense foliage's intricately layered habitats. Wild inhabitants of other environments have also been hard hit by such changes. The fencing of a grassland may place a frustrating constraint on the freedom of movement of large migratory grazers. The damming of a river affects not only the residents evicted from the inundated valley but also the

Coyote on the grounds of the Arizona-Sonora Desert Museum outside of Tucson

shallow-water fish, which cannot survive in a deep lake, and the animals downstream that may find their water supply cut to a brackish trickle. The draining or filling of a marsh takes away the homes and breeding grounds for scores of amphibians and waterfowl, as well as the food supply for many small predators.

The introduction of animals not native to a region also frequently upsets the delicate balance of nature. In this regard, by far the greatest destruction has been wrought by domestic livestock. Cattle and sheep do not graze as efficiently on marginal terrain as the animals that over thousands of years have adapted themselves to such an area's meager resources. As a result the new arrivals often strip the land of its protective grass and leave a wind-eroded desert. Vast tracts of central Australia and large parts of the American Great Plains have been damaged in this way. Other alien intruders have also created their share of problems. Rabbits brought into Australia, where they had no natural enemies, proliferated so fast that they threatened to drive out many of that continent's unique animals. Mongooses introduced into the West Indies to control the islands' rats and snakes quickly decimated their intended prey and took after the local birds, including the natives' chickens. Changes in animal populations caused by man have created other disastrous imbalances. The shooting of wildcats and owls in Brazil brought on a dangerous explosion of diseased rats, and the poaching of alligators in Argentina resulted in unfordable rivers teeming with piranhas.

Such destruction has obvious medical and social implications. There are other considerations. "If someone went out and destroyed a Rembrandt," remarks a scientist on the staff of the World Wildlife Fund, "everyone would scream. But by destroying species, you're doing the same thing in an esthetic sense." It is no wonder that esthetics, among other things, helps explain the origins of animal preservation. From the dawn of civilization, kings and emperors viewed captive animals as symbols of their own appreciation of beauty, and of their culture, wealth and dominance. Royal menageries were even regarded occasionally as sources of scientific knowledge. Unfortunately, the ferocity of some wild animals also led to their exploitation under royal auspices as adversaries—in fights to the death with one another or with men.

Egyptian tomb pictures from the 25th century B.C. show antelopes wearing collars—an indication that they had been captured or bred in captivity. A later Egyptian monarch, Queen Hatshepsut, sent an expedition to the land of Punt (probably what is now Somalia) that returned with monkeys, greyhounds, exotic birds—and wonder of wonders— a giraffe. Around 1000 B.C. the Chinese Emperor Wen Wang established a 1,500-acre park for creatures brought from all parts of his empire, named it "Garden of Intelligence," and filled in with deer, fishes and "white birds with dazzling plumes."

Although many important persons of ancient times kept or collected animals primarily for show or combat, the Greeks were beginning to study them in the seventh century B.C. By the fourth century B.C., few self-respecting Greek city-states lacked a well-stocked animal collection and no one could claim to be educated without learning what it had to teach. In this atmosphere Aristotle found great encouragement for his studies, which produced his monumental *History of*

In this 1835 lithograph, an elephant and a caged lion rescue J. Martin, keeper of New York's Bowery Menagerie, from attack by two escaped leopards. The elephant is described in the original caption as magnanimous, and the spotted cats are identified as tigers—an indication of their strangeness to contemporary North Americans.

Animals—a description of 300 species of vertebrates that can be clearly identified from his data today.

In their great arenas the Romans probably promoted the slaughter of animals in combat further than any other peoples before or since. In the Roman Colosseum of the second century A.D., 485,000 people could roar with bloodlust as lions and tigers tore each other—or human victims—to pieces. In fairness, such Romans as Varro and Pliny the Elder followed a more studious course: Varro kept a collection

of half-wild animals on the grounds of his villa and Pliny wrote a natural-history book that is still worth reading.

The medieval kings of Europe continued the tradition of the animal collection as a demonstration of pomp and power. In this spirit, Henry III of England established a zoo in the Tower of London in the 13th century and imported the first elephant ever seen in the British Isles. He also sponsored fights between lions and tigers billed as contests between rival contenders for the title "King of Beasts." Continuing the tradition in more genteel fashion, France's Louis XIV arranged the quarters of the animals in his royal menagerie in the form of a wheel with spokes fanning out from a central hub. He also concealed the harsh outlines of cages and enclosures

with plantings of shrubs, trees and flowers—the genesis of the "zoological garden." It was soon after his grandson Louis XVI had been sent to the guillotine by the new revolutionary rulers of France that the royal menagerie was transplanted to Paris and opened to the public by government decree. One of the earliest experiments in animal psychology was conducted there in 1798: Scientists noted the reactions of an elephant as it was being serenaded by an orchestra. The big animal is said to have swayed rhythmically with the march music, registered annoyance at the blasts of brass instruments and slept through the symphonic passages.

Relatively uncommon in today's zoo scene, music almost always has been associated with the circus, as have elephants. From earliest times the word *circus* has been linked with animals—particularly wild animals. Though some of them were trained, they were always known as wild animals, and that always meant lions and tigers, leopards, jaguars and bears. Circus acts involving such animals were so widely criticized that Ringling Brothers, Barnum & Bailey, the biggest and best-known American circus, suspended them for four years during the '20s on the

12

general grounds that the circus customers felt they were too cruel, violent and dangerous. As Charles Ringling put it, "the public seems to prefer animal acts in which the animals themselves seem to take an interested and playful part, as do dogs, seals, horses, elephants, etc." Ringling Brothers resumed the lion acts in 1925, and has continued them to this day—with highly skilled trainers and the best possible care for animals living outside the wild.

As for the animals still living in the wilderness, the first real impetus to protect them and their whole environment, for no other reason than their innate worth, originated in North America. In a measure signed by President Abraham Lincoln in 1864, the magnificent Yosemite Valley became the first federal land to be set aside as a national park, and in 1872 the enormous two-million-acre tract in the geyser-filled Yellowstone region of the Wyoming territory was given the same status. Although both Yosemite and Yellowstone were set up primarily to protect scenic wonders, they soon became totally protected animal refuges after the shocking near demise of the bison in the late 19th century. In those years the active lobbying of naturalists like John Muir, the founder of the Sierra Club, who preached the gospel of wilderness preservation with the evangelical fervor of a prophet, dovetailed with the enlightened policies of President Theodore Roosevelt. The result, in the early 1900s, was an extensive system of parks and other protected areas, such as the Badlands National Monument in the Dakotas (pages 54–55).

This 1891 poster advertises one of Barnum and Bailey's earlier extravaganzas. While most of these animals—then an unusual sight in the U.S.—probably did not actually perform, the tour included circus acts involving horses and elephants.

During this century a few other countries, most notably Canada, Australia, Switzerland and the Union of South Africa, also undertook the task of preserving their dwindling wilderness. For the men who were pioneering the new concept of preservation, the obstacles could be severe. One hurdle was the apathy or the downright hostility of the public. "Would it be possible," lamented J. Stevenson-Hamilton, an early South African park superintendent, "to wean the South African public from its present attitude towards the wild animals of its own country . . . regarding them either as a convenient source of exploitation or an incubus hindering the progress of civilization? It seemed," he concluded, "pretty hopeless. . . ." Another difficulty would be a shortage of money, even when the government was sympathetic. As Stevenson-Hamilton reported, "At the commencement of each financial year, I gave a sigh of relief when I found our small grant of £5,000 still on the estimates, a sum which barely sufficed to pay salaries and wages, with nothing left over to construct dwellings for the staff, or to carry out the hundred and one improvements I had in mind." Fortunately, men like Stevenson-Hamilton were believers, convinced that it was worth it to try "to increase our depleted fauna, hoping that some day it might be recognized as a definite asset; as something that was more admirable alive than dead."

Despair for the wildlife of Africa reached a peak in the late 1950s when experts issued dire warnings that the imminent independence of African countries would result in the total destruction of their vast animal populations within a few years. The predictions proved untrue, however, and some African governments proved to be more dedicated and effective in the preservation of their wildlife heritage than their colonial predecessors.

Regardless of such encouraging signs, dedication is still necessary. Havens like national parks are still vulnerable, for instance, to public opposition: The last Asiatic lions occupy a reserve in the Gir Forest in India that is adjacent to the pasturage of domestic cattle owned by people who would like to see the lions exterminated. Nevertheless, the concept of preserves seems to be an idea whose time has finally come—though perhaps it has arrived too late. It was only after the end of World War II that national parks and other refuges began to proliferate throughout the world. But in their short history, preserves have had a remarkable success in saving animals that were near extinction. They include the great bison of the American plains as well as its less well known but more endangered cousin, the European bison, once common in Poland and Russia. In southern Africa, the list includes the white rhinoceros and the Cape mountain zebra as well as the bontebok and black wildebeest antelopes.

At an estimated height of 11 feet 2 inches at the shoulder and a weight of over six and a half tons, Jumbo was the largest elephant in captivity. Acquired by the London Zoological Gardens in 1865, Jumbo was sold to P.T. Barnum in 1882—a transfer of ownership that outraged the elephant's loyal British fans.

Despite their increased numbers and outstanding successes, preserves still face many problems, especially in the developing regions of the world where governments lack the funds to protect enclaves from poachers, loggers, herdsmen and other intruders. At the same time these nations are under increasing pressure to surrender these last few remaining pockets of wilderness to farmers and ranchers so that they can feed their growing populations. And there is also a serious dearth of well-protected refuges in the great tropical rain forests like the Amazon River basin, which is increasingly losing its unparalleled collection of exotic birds and monkeys to pet dealers. Indeed, only the first few skirmishes in the fight to save the world's wildlife have been won, and a continually renewed effort will always be needed to assure that their survival is not just a passing event.

The 18th century Italian artist Pietro Longhi is best known for his paintings of scenes from the lives of the bourgeois and upper classes. In Exhibition of a Rhinoceros at Venice (opposite), Longhi depicts a group of Venetians observing an animal feeding. Some of the spectators are wearing masks, a custom during carnival.

14

Zoos

For many people zoos are simply a pleasant place to take a Sunday outing—a place where the casual stroller can be amused by the almost human antics of chimpanzees, chilled by a boa constrictor and awed by the graceful majesty of a great lion crossing a simulated African veld. But what most visitors fail to realize is that at a modern zoo more varieties of animals can be observed at closer range than on a trek to the most untamed regions of the globe. Taken together, today's zoos constitute one of the world's greatest wildlife preserves.

The London Zoo, founded in 1828, has particularly emphasized comprehensiveness and scholarship, and is regarded as having achieved the greatest distinction among early modern zoos. The popular attraction in Regent's Park also gave zoos their name when the British, with a penchant for catchy concision that had already clipped "public house" to "pub," quickly pruned "zoological garden" to "zoo." Before the end of the century, most major cities in Europe and America opened zoos, including Amsterdam, Antwerp, Berlin, Washington and New York.

Most of these 19th century zoological showcases boasted beautifully manicured grounds and often fanciful structures. Berlin built a pavilion in an Arabian motif for its zebras and a Persian structure for its wild horses. London housed its reptiles in a Swiss chalet and Frankfurt used candy-striped tents for its camels and llamas. But unfortunately these edifices did little to meet the real needs of their occupants. Throughout most of the year, the majority of the animals were locked up inside cramped cages in buildings that were usually poorly ventilated and overheated; many animals suffered because of the mistaken belief that any creature from the tropics would expire if exposed for long to a cold draft. And at a time when much still remained to be learned about sanitation, the houses were far from hygienic. Not surprisingly, the first chimp introduced into London in 1835 died within six months; the next one, arriving in 1845, survived less than a year. And it was not until World War I that chimps or any other apes lived much longer in captivity.

The radical transformation of zoos from the jailhouse atmosphere of the last century to the freer ambience commoner today is largely the doing of one man, Carl Hagenbeck. The world's leading animal dealer in Europe during the 1880s and owner of a popular circus, Hagenbeck understood animals and had a sympathy for them that was then uncommon in either of his trades. He knew that in winter large mammals needed fresh air and freedom of movement more than heat, and that most could acclimatize quite well if they had a sheltered retreat. He also felt that they should be placed in an environment without bars, one that bore the closest possible resemblance to their own native habitats. He put his ideas into action when he opened a zoo in Stellingen on the outskirts of Hamburg in 1907. To keep predator apart from prey Hagenbeck devised an ingenious maze of deep trenches and water-filled moats that were often landscaped so that they were virtually invisible. In his African panorama, the gazelles, cranes and flamingos in the foregound, as well as the antelopes and zebras just beyond them, seemed to be on the same plain as the lions, which were still farther away. Far in the background, from the spectator's viewpoint, rocky promontories were inhabited by wild sheep and ibex.

To a great extent nearly every major zoo employs Hagenbeck's approach. With modern technology, however, many zoos have gone much further. They have created vast enclosures where varying conditions of temperature, humidity, soil and vegetation reproduce habitats ranging from rain forests to deserts. Environment control is especially important to such climate-sensitive animals as reptiles and small mammals. Day and night have been reversed in some exhibits so that owls, bats and other nocturnal creatures can be observed in action during the day. For birds, dreary cage-lined rooms have been replaced by vaulting walk-through, fly-through aviaries. And some city-bound zoos, most notably London's and San Diego's, have created spacious annexes in nearby rural regions.

With improved conditions and a better understanding of animal behavior, zoos also have had remarkable success in breeding new populations of such rare animals as the cheetah; and in a widely acclaimed breeding achievement, the first African elephant ever born in captivity in the New World was delivered at the Knoxville, Tennessee, zoo early in 1978. Zoos provide havens for nearly all endangered species, and for some near-extinct animals they are the last refuge. Zoos play a crucial role in spreading concern for the conservation of wildlife: If they did not bring home a glimpse of the reality of life for wild animals, far fewer people would be aware of these creatures; fewer still would be knowledgeable about the troubles of some—and the sheer desperation of others.

Penguins at the San Diego Zoo

Meerkats, which are not felines, are sociable relatives of the mongoose, with a special fondness for sunbathing. To make them feel more at home in the chilly German climate, the zoo provides a sunlamp (left).

A male aardwolf (below) playfully stalks his crouching mate in a Frankfurt facsimile of their native southern African grassland habitat. Aardwolves are unrelated to wolves, but closely related to hyenas.

Rebirth in Frankfurt

The Frankfurt Zoo in West Germany was 100 years old in 1958, but the fact that it survived at all is due to Dr. Bernhard Grzimek, a veterinarian, noted zoologist and entrepreneur who became its director in 1946. Devastated during World War II, the zoo's population had shrunk from its prewar peak of a substantial number of specimens to a meager score of animals. By staging circuses and operas in the park grounds, Grzimek was able to raise enough money to rebuild the Frankfurt Tiergarten and to turn it into one of Europe's showplace zoos. As a conservator of rare animals, Frankfurt has had a notably successful record in breeding orangutans, maned wolves, okapis and the threatened Af-

rican animals shown on these pages.

Having rehabilitated the Frankfurt Zoo, the peripatetic Dr. Grzimek turned his attention to other notable services: field research and conservation. His studies in the 1950s of the wildlife of Serengeti National Park in Tanzania, plus his fund raising, publicizing and publishing, made that pristine preserve famous and helped it to survive. Then, with the aid of nearly 200 scientists, he compiled a comprehensive 13-volume encyclopedia of the earth's fauna that was published in 1970. However, the Frankfurt Zoo is perhaps the best testimonial to his energetic efforts on behalf of the world's wildlife.

As a youngster Snowflake (left) readily took to the swings, rubber tires and other playthings provided by his keepers. He shared his special cage with two normal dark-furred lowland gorillas his own age. But as the three grew older, Snowflake and Muni, the other male, fought for the affection of Endengui, the young female. Snowflake's rival was banished and Endengui became the white primate's first mate.

Although his eyes are blue rather than pink, Snowflake (opposite) is a true albino. His black-coated mother was killed during his capture, and the tiny gorilla was bottle-fed and raised by human foster parents. Primatologists doubt that Snowflake could ever have grown to adulthood in the wild: Other gorillas would almost certainly have rejected him, and his chances of surviving as a conspicuous platinum-blond loner in the jungle would be slim.

Barcelona's Star

Located in a large 19th century park, the Parque Zoologico is one of Barcelona's most popular tourist attractions, drawing four million visitors each year, the greatest attendance for any zoo in Europe. The zoo is renowned for its collection of African animals, which are displayed in a spectacular succession of islands, each with its special denizens usually housed in pairs.

The star attraction in the Barcelona Zoo, however, is Copito de Nieve (Snowflake), the only known white gorilla in the world. Ever since his arrival in Spain in 1966 as a wistful little orphan from the jungles of Equatorial Guinea, Snowflake has excited the interest of scientists, photographers and children. Now a sedate adult, weighing more than 250 pounds, he has fathered several babies, none of them albinos. But scientists hope that eventually he will start a line that could produce more white apes.

Profitable Preservation in Basel

The Basel Zoological Garden is modestly sized, run with typical Swiss efficiency and famous for its successful breeding of rare animals. Located in the heart of the city, the zoo is small enough to be seen in an hour, and the Swiss agree that it provides the best show in town. Although it is over 100 years old, the Basel Zoo, like everything else in neutral Switzerland, has never suffered from the ravages of the wars that have periodically devastated European zoos.

Soon after World War II Dr. Ernst Lang, an eminent veterinarian, concluded that the zoo should be more than just an assortment of exhibitions, and instituted a policy of selectively breeding threatened species of animals. Basel has been the scene of the birth of the second gorilla ever born in captivity (first honors go to the Columbus, Ohio, zoo), the first hatching of a king penguin egg in Europe, and is a major hope for the survival of the Indian rhino. Basel's animal husbandry program has been financially as well as biologically successful and helps pay the zoo's expenses: A bred-in-Basel Indian rhino at the age of one year may bring a price from another zoo of $24,000.

Wherever possible the zoo's animals mingle freely with human visitors; the unperturbed king penguins (right) are being taken for a constitutional down a public walk. The zoo also recognizes that some animals need privacy and provides secluded areas where they can relax.

The polar bear below would appear to be in its arctic element, except for the human intruders. The Basel Zoo has been especially successful in making northern animals feel at home away from home. Recent acquisitions include Alaskan musk oxen.

23

Menagerie Manor

by Gerald Durrell

An irrepressible collector of animals since childhood, Gerald Durrell, seen below with a leopard cub, had a lifelong dream of establishing a zoo of his own. In 1957 he realized that dream with the establishment of the Jersey Wildlife Preservation Trust on the island of Jersey in the English Channel. The Trust is dedicated to the preservation of endangered species and is home to more than 500 animals—including Claudius, a South American tapir with a penchant for midnight peregrinations. Menagerie Manor *is the story of one such stroll.*

There are again some creatures, of course, which, when they manage to escape, present you with considerable problems. For instance, there was the night I shall never forget, when Claudius, the South American tapir, contrived to find a way out of his paddock. The person who had been in to give him his night feed had padlocked the gate carefully but without sliding the bolt into position. Claudius, having a nocturnal perambulation round his territory, found to his delight that the gate which he had hitherto presumed to be invulnerable now responded to his gentle nosings. He decided that this was a very suitable

night to have a short incursion into the neighbouring countryside. It was a suitable night from Claudius's point of view, because the skies were as black as pitch and the rain was streaming down in torrents that I have rarely seen equalled outside the tropics.

It was about quarter past eleven, and we were all on the point of going to bed, when a rather harassed and extremely wet motorist appeared and beat upon the front door. Above the roar of the rain, he said that he had just seen a big animal in the headlights of his car, which he felt sure must be one of ours. I asked him what it looked like, and he said it looked to him like a misshapen Shetland pony with an elephant's trunk. My heart sank, for I knew just how far and how fast Claudius could gallop if given half a chance. I was in my shirt-sleeves and only wearing slippers, but there was no time to change into more suitable attire against the weather, for the motorist had spotted Claudius in a field adjoining our property and I wanted to catch up with him before he ventured too far afield. I rushed round to the cottage and harried all those members of the staff who lived in. In various stages of night attire they all tumbled out into the rain and we headed for the field into which the motorist assured us our tapir had disappeared. This was quite a large field and belonged to our nearest neighbour, Leonard du Feu. Leonard had proved himself to be the most long suffering and sympathetic of neighbours, and so I was determined that Claudius was not going to do any damage to his property if we could possibly avoid it. Having made this mental resolve, I then remembered to my horror that the field in which Claudius was reputedly lurking had just recently been carefully planted out by Leonard with anemones. I could imagine what Claudius's four hundred-weight could do to those carefully planted rows of delicate plants, particularly as, owing to his short-sightedness, his sense of direction was never too good at the best of times.

We reached the field, soaked to the skin, and surrounded it. There, sure enough, stood Claudius obviously having the best evening out he had had in years. The wet as far as he was concerned was ideal: there was nothing quite like a heavy downpour of rain to make life worth while. He was standing there, looking like a debauched Roman emperor under a shower, meditatively masticating a large bunch of

anemones. When he saw us, he uttered his greeting—a ridiculous, high-pitched squeak similar to the noise of a wet finger being rubbed over a balloon. It was quite plain that he was delighted to see us and hoped that we would join him in his nocturnal ramble, but none of us was feeling in any mood to do this. We were drenched to the skin and freezing cold, and our one ambition was to get Claudius back into his paddock with as little trouble as possible. Uttering a despairing and rather futile cry of 'don't tread on the plants', I marshalled my band of tapir-catchers and we converged on Claudius in a grim-faced

body. Claudius took one look at us and decided from our manner and bearing that we did not see eye to eye with him on the subject of gambolling about in other people's fields at half past eleven on a wet night, and so he felt that, albeit reluctantly, he would have to leave us. Pausing only to snatch another mouthful of anemones, he set off across the field at a sharp gallop, leaving a trail of destruction behind him that could only have been emulated by a runaway bulldozer. In our slippered feet, clotted with mud, we stumbled after him. Our speed was reduced not only by the mud but by the fact that we were trying to run between the rows of flowers instead of on them. I remember making a mental note as I ran that I would ask Leonard in future to plant his rows of flowers wider apart, as this would facilitate the recapture of any animal that escaped. The damage Claudius had done to the flowers was bad enough, but worse was to follow. He suddenly swerved, and instead of running into the next field, as we had hoped (for it was a grazing meadow), he ran straight into Leonard du Feu's back-garden. We pulled up short and stood panting, the rain trickling off us in torrents.

'For God's sake,' I said to everyone in general, 'get that bloody animal out of that garden before he wrecks it.' The words were hardly out of my mouth when from inside the garden came a series of tinkling crashes which told us too clearly that Claudius, trotting along in his normal myopic fashion, had ploughed his way through all Leonard's

cloches. Before we could do anything sensible, Claudius having decided that Leonard's garden was not to his liking, crashed his way through a hedge, leaving a gaping hole in what hitherto had been a nice piece of topiary, and set off into the night at a brisk trot. The direction he was taking presented yet another danger, for he was heading straight for our small lake. Tapirs in the wild state are very fond of water and they are excellent swimmers and can submerge themselves for a considerable length of time. The thought of having to search for a tapir in a quarter of an acre of dark water on a pitch black, rainy night made the thought of hunting for a needle in a haystack pale into insignificance. This thought struck the other members of my band at the same moment, and we ran as we had never run before and just succeeded at the very last minute in heading off Claudius. Coming up close to his rotund behind, I

launched myself in a flying tackle and, more by luck than judgement, managed to grab him by one hind leg. In thirty seconds I was wishing that I had not. Claudius kicked out and caught me a glancing blow on the side of the head, which made me see stars, and then revved up to a gallop, dragging me ignominiously through the mud, but by now I was so wet, so cold, so muddy and so angry that I clung on with the determination of a limpet in a storm. My tenacity was rewarded, for my dragging weight slowed Claudius down sufficiently to allow the others to catch up, and they hurled themselves on various portions of his anatomy. The chief difficulty with a tapir is that there is practically nothing on which to hold: the ears are small and provide a precarious grip, the tail is minute, there is no mane, so really the only part you can grip with any degree of success are its legs, and Claudius's legs were fat and slippery with rain. However, we all clung on grimly, while he bucked and kicked and snorted indignantly. As one person loosened his hold, another one would grab on until eventually Claudius decided he was using the wrong method of discouragement. He stopped pirouetting about, thought to himself for a moment and then just simply lay down and looked at us.

We stood round him in a sodden, exhausted circle and looked at each other. There were five of us and four hundredweight of reluctant tapir. It was beyond our powers to carry him, and yet it was quite obvious that Claudius had no intention of helping us in any way. He lay there with a mulish expression on his face. If we wanted to get him back to the Zoo, it implied, we would jolly well have to carry him. We had no more reinforcements to call on, and so it appeared that we had reached an impasse. However, as Claudius was prepared to be stubborn, I was prepared to be equally so. I sent one of my dripping team back to the Zoo for a rope. I should, of course, have brought this very necessary adjunct of capture with me, but in my innocence I had assumed that Claudius could be chivied back to his paddock with no more trouble than a domestic goat. When the rope arrived, we attached it firmly round Claudius's neck, making sure that it was not a slip-knot. I thought one drenched member of the staff was heard to mutter that a slip-knot would be ideal. Then two of us took hold of the rope, two more took hold of his ears,

and the fifth took hold of his hind legs, and by the application of considerable exertion we raised him to his feet and wheel-barrowed him all of ten feet, before he collapsed again. We had a short pause to regain our breath and started off again. Once more we carted him for about ten feet, in the process of which I lost a slipper and had my hand heavily trodden on by one of the larger and weightier members of my team. We rested again, sitting dejectedly and panting in the rain, longing for a cigarette and unanimously deciding that tapirs were animals that should never in any circumstances have been invented.

The field in which these operations took place was large and muddy. At that hour of night, under the stinging rain, it resembled an ancient tank-training ground which had been abandoned because the tanks could no longer get through it. The mud in it appeared to have a glue-like quality not found elsewhere in the Island of Jersey. It took us an hour and a half to get Claudius out of that field, and at the end of it we felt rather like those people must have felt who erected Stonehenge—that none of us was ruptured was a miracle. A final colossal effort and we hauled Claudius out of the field and over the boundary into the Zoo. Here we were going to pause for further recuperation, but Claudius decided that since we had brought him back into the Zoo grounds and would, it appeared, inevitably return him to his paddock, it would be silly to delay. He suddenly rose to his feet and took off like a rocket, all of us desperately clinging to various parts of his body. It seemed ludicrous that for an hour and a half we should have been making the valiant attempt to get him to move at all and now we were clinging to his fat body in an effort to slow him down for fear that in his normal blundering way he would run full tilt into one of the granite archways and hurt or perhaps even kill himself. We clung to him like sucker-fish to a speeding shark, and, to our intense relief, managed to steer our irritating vehicle back into its paddock, without any further mishap, and so we returned to our respective bedrooms, bruised, cold and covered with mud. I had a hot bath to recuperate, but as I lay in it drowsily, I reflected that the worst was yet to come: the following morning I had to telephone Leonard du Feu and try to apologize for half an acre of trampled anemones and twelve broken cloches.

Addaxes (below) are an endangered species, and those at Hai Bar South are descended from three specimens purchased with a $10,000 donation from a game preserve in New York's Catskill Mountains. Hai Bar South now has more than 300 species of animals that have been introduced or reestablished in its habitat.

Somali wild asses (right) gallop across the Negev sands. These hardy, handsome animals were brought from Ethiopia and are part of Hai Bar South's 15-member herd, the only one in captivity. They have successfully reproduced—proof that the wild asses have adapted well to their new home.

Ark of the Desert

A collection of the birds and beasts that roamed the Holy Land during biblical times is being assembled in the arid expanses of the Negev desert. The wildlife reserve known as Hai Bar South is supported chiefly by private donations, and occupies an 8,000-acre tract with few fences to contain the animals, most of them species that populated the area when it was a well-forested Old Testament land of milk and honey.

Under the direction of Mike van Grevenbroek, a Dutch zoologist, Hai Bar South has regained much of its Old Testament character. From all over the world, contributors have sent such species as ostriches, fallow deer, addaxes (opposite), onagers and Somali wild asses. Ibexes, ancestors of the domestic goat, usually inhabit rugged mountain country, but those in the reserve have acclimated to their new environment with the help of boulders trucked in from an abandoned copper mine. One of Hai Bar South's most valued nonbiblical animals is the scimitar-horned Saharan oryx, which has become extinct in its North African habitat. Although the oryx is not considered a biblical animal, it represents another feature of Hai Bar South's overall plan to protect desert species of the region.

A leopard cat (below) peers out from its enclosure. In the wild this cat begins to hunt for small mammals and birds as soon as it gets dark, and stays inactive in its den during the day. It maintains this pattern in the zoo even though it no longer must hunt to eat.

A slow loris (opposite) moves along a branch with a steady hand-over-hand pace. Like most primates, the loris has opposable digits and uses them to grasp a branch when climbing. The loris can move upside down beneath the branch just as easily as on top of it.

Day into Night

The Bronx Zoo's House of Darkness is an exhibit of nocturnal animals that is just one example of the zoo's effort to show animals in their natural environment. During the day some animals are exhibited under red light, which seems to them like darkness but gives zoo visitors a clear view of their activities. Toward evening the light brightens as in daylight, and the animals go to sleep.

Among the exhibit's leading residents are the leopard cat and the slow loris. A native of Asia, the cat is not only an agile climber but also an excellent and willing swimmer. However, it is best known for its bad temper.

The enormous eyes of the slow loris may give this native of Southeast Asia a comical appearance, but they function superbly in the dark. In the wild the slow loris is omnivorous, and it creeps up on any insect or other small creature that wanders close by. In the zoo the lazy loris seems to be perfectly content on a diet of fruit, mealworms and canned dog food.

A Living Museum

The Arizona-Sonora Desert Museum west of Tucson is not a conventional museum or zoo, but an unusual and successful establishment that demonstrates the interplay between wildlife and the desert environment. All the animals are indigenous to the area and are seen in their natural environment or against dioramas that approximate the regional ecology. The museum's outdoor terrain, in Tucson Mountain Park, ranges from desert plains to mountain woodlands and has a corresponding variety of wildlife.

Birds, fish, amphibians and small mammals, such as the two shown here, are all represented in the museum.

The mainly carnivorous ringtail, or cacomistle (above), is a nocturnal relative of the raccoon. It averages three feet in length, half of which is a fluffy, ringed tail. The omnivorous coatimundi, or "chulu bear," travels in a tree-climbing band and forages during daylight hours. Unlike the shy ringtail, the coatimundi is easy to spot even in the wild and is a favorite of museum visitors.

A ringtail (left) rests in a tree away from the hot midday sun. This shy predator waits until sunset to make its hunting forays for small animals, birds and insects. It has a sharp, barking cry that pierces the stillness of the night.

Looking like a bear cub, a coatimundi balances precariously (right) atop a small desert shrub. Its anatomy is a hodgepodge. The snout is hedgehog-like, the ringed eye mask is like that of a raccoon and the canine teeth would do a wolf proud.

Second Chance

Home to 1,100 different species and subspecies of animals, with a total population of over 4,000, the San Diego Zoo and its adjunct, the Wild Animal Park (pages 36–37) have the largest collection of terrestrial animals in the United States.

Of these animals more than 100 species are officially classified as rare or endangered, and as a result the San Diego facility has become one of the foremost breeding institutions in the world, in the forefront of the fight to save animals threatened with extinction. For example, Przewalski's horse (below), believed to be extinct in its native Mongolia, exists only in zoos like the San Diego.

Last year alone some 54 species of mammals reproduced successfully at the San Diego Zoo, including the shy and wary stripe-legged okapi (left). The animals born at the zoo serve various purposes. Some are sold or traded to other zoos, creating revenue that contributes a large percentage of the approximately $100,000 budget the San Diego Zoo sets aside annually for the acquisition of new species. And a few animals are earmarked for eventual return to a life in their original wild habitats.

An okapi mother nurses her youngster in their cage at the San Diego Zoo (opposite). Although okapis were plentiful in their native central Africa, they were unknown to naturalists before 1900.

A handsome adult gorilla (right), resident at the San Diego Zoo, represents a menaced species. Extensive deforestation is rapidly eliminating the great apes' native habitat, and San Diego has reacted with plans to build a major primate breeding center.

A small breeding herd of Przewalski's horses congregates in zoo enclosure (below). The San Diego Zoo has had much success breeding these animals, which are the only true wild horses, and has logged a total of seven births.

San Diego's Savanna Success

Similar to the savannas of Africa, the 1,800 acres of the San Diego Zoo's Wild Animal Park, established in 1972, provide an ideal haven for the breeding of animals whose wild habitats are dwindling. Many animals do not breed easily in captivity, and many refuse to mate at all. Yet the zoo has been able to achieve good results after conducting extensive research on mating habits in the wild and attempting to duplicate the natural circumstances of reproduction.

Both cheetahs and rhinos have always been particularly difficult to breed in captivity. In ancient times when Indian princes trained cheetahs to hunt, they were constantly capturing replacements from the wild because their tame cheetahs refused to mate. The African white rhinoceros even in the wild gives birth to only one offspring every two years, and zoologists have feared it would soon be extinct. However, by applying its field data on cheetah and rhino breeding behavior, the Wild Animal Park has been able to breed both successfully. And the giraffes (overleaf), which mate readily in captivity, have had healthier babies as a result of the research.

A cheetah (above) keeps close watch on her cubs and at the same time instinctively searches her surroundings for potential prey. The cheetahs raise their cubs just as they would in the wild, bringing them out of the den to feed—a safety measure to keep the lair's location secret.

Several African white rhinos stir up dust (left) while irritably charging each other. These three-ton grass eaters are actually gray-brown, but get the name "white" from the Afrikaans word "weit," meaning wide and referring to their mouths.

A group of giraffes (overleaf) leaves a watering hole, having drunk enough to last them for weeks. To drink, giraffes must spread their forelegs wide apart and bend their long necks to the water, which they lap up in hearty drafts with their 12- to 18-inch tongues.

American Grasslands

Bounded on the north by the dense forests of central Canada and on the south by the arid cactus country of Texas and New Mexico, the Great Plains are an enormous elevated grassland located almost exactly in the center of the North American continent. From its eastern edge along the Mississippi Valley, the upland prairie is dotted with numerous preserves westward as far as the foothills of the Rockies. It is a land of harsh climatic extremes. The summer sun, sizzling in a cloudless sky, often raises the temperature to over 100° F. In winter the frigid air of the prevailing westerlies drops the thermometer to below zero; sudden plunges of 40° are common. Rain and snow are infrequent—only about 16 inches a year—but when they do come it is often from a violent cloudburst or a lethal blizzard. The layer of fertile topsoil is thin; except for some patches of cottonwood along the riverbanks and scrub pine on the north slope of hills, the only vegetation that thrives naturally is an array of hardy grasses and weeds.

As forbidding as it may seem, this land once harbored a vast quantity of wildlife. Most numerous, at least to the eyes of early explorers, were bison, the shaggy lords of this newfound land. Since a bull stands taller than a man and weighs more than a ton, it is no wonder that witnesses were impressed as a thousand head rumbled by at 35 miles an hour. As late as the 1860s, there were an estimated 60 million of these huge creatures roaming the continent.

The bison were not alone. There were also enormous herds of deer and elk, as well as pronghorn, the fleet-footed animals often mistakenly called antelopes. And these hoofed creatures shared their grazing grounds with an even greater number of smaller mammals such as pocket gophers, badgers, jackrabbits, cottontails and deer mice. One of the most abundant was a lively rodent unique to the terrain—the prairie dog. Like most small animals on the plains, prairie dogs survive the extremes of the climate by digging homes deep in the earth. These burrows usually have at least two entrances, each surrounded by a conical mound of earth. At one time the mounds constructed by these sociable creatures could be seen stretching over areas of several square miles. The prairie dogs' abodes served as retreats from a fearsome collection of predators—coyotes, foxes, bobcats and badgers that prowled the plains, as well as hawks and eagles soaring above. However, the burrows gave little protection against the slender-bodied black-footed ferret, which could slip smoothly and quickly into a prairie dog's long tunnel. And they could not deter bull snakes, rattlers and burrowing owls looking for a home as well as a meal.

As late as 1850, the Great Plains still teemed with wildlife. The next few decades, however, witnessed a swift and tragic destruction of animal life on a scale almost without parallel. The great herds went first, killed off not only by hunters seeking hides and meat and by ranchers seeking new ranges but also by heedless transients—soldiers and railroaders—and by Indians seeking food. Bison, the main target, were reduced by the 1890s from tens of millions to under 300. The pronghorn's decline was almost equally precipitous. With homesteaders following the ranchers onto the plains, smaller animals were most often wiped out by the destruction of their habitat. Both farmers and cattlemen diligently cleared their land of the ubiquitous prairie dog, whose burrows broke the legs of livestock, and nearly everybody subscribed to the prairie notion that coyotes and bobcats were varmints to be shot on sight.

Although the turnabout was slow, the survival of most of the animals of the plains seems to be assured. Since the turn of the century, bison have increased to 35,000 in North America and pronghorn number well over a half million. After three quarters of a century of concerted effort by conservationists, the American West boasts one of the most extensive series of preserves in the world—including many in the Rockies and other areas bordering the Great Plains that shelter much of the upland's wild inhabitants.

On the Great Plains themselves, however, the greatest concentration of sanctuaries is in the western Dakotas—a land noted for the fierce beauty of the long stretches of severely eroded terrain called the Badlands. Along the paths of many rivers and creeks in this region, nature has sculpted a jagged tableau of buttes, mesas, gullies and gulches. The best known parks—the Badlands National Monument in South Dakota and the two branches of the Theodore Roosevelt National Memorial Park in North Dakota—were set up to protect this scenic wonder as well as wildlife. But these two parks are only a small part of a network of refuges, national forests, grasslands Indian reservations and other federally protected lands in both states. In all, several hundred square miles have been set aside. And in one of conservation's great success stories, many of the original wild species—especially deer and pronghorn—have staged a dramatic comeback.

Prairie dog

Groups of prairie dog pups (above, top and bottom) forage contentedly near the entrance to their burrows. Pups are born between March and May but do not leave their subterranean nests until June, when they have been weaned.

The boundless energy of three young prairie dogs (opposite) is displayed in an enthusiastic wrestling match. Tussles like this provide both a form of strength-building exercise and an early introduction to social behavior.

Secure Beginnings

The extended nuclear family is alive and well in the prairie dog towns of the American Midwest. The towns may have several thousand inhabitants spread over a 160-acre area and are made up of volcano-shaped burrows (pages 44–45). These burrows are home to family groups called coteries, which generally consist of a single male, several females and a half dozen youngsters.

At birth a prairie dog pup enters a world filled with warmth, affection and security. While adult prairie dogs are barred as intruders from all but their own burrows, pups are accepted everywhere they wander. Nursing females suckle any pup that approaches them, and all adults, male and female, nuzzle and groom them virtually on demand. A pup must push an adult pretty far to receive even the mildest rebuff, and most adults will choose to leave rather than play the role of disciplinarian.

As the pups mature, however, they conform to adult ways. While females are often absorbed into their original groups, males vie with the lead male for dominance; if defeated, they go off to form coteries of their own.

Prairie Home Developers

Prairie dog towns are marvels of architecture, each burrow providing its inhabitants a variety of modern conveniences ranging from insulation to air conditioning. The average 10- to 15-foot depth of the burrows ensures a fairly constant interior temperature all year long, keeping the animals cool in summer, when 100° F. days are not uncommon, and warm in the winter, when many prairie dogs go into partial hibernation, especially those in the northernmost parts of their range, where winter weather is especially severe. A few days of clear, sunny weather, however, will bring these hardy creatures out again, even in the dead of winter.

The entrance to each burrow is encircled with a lip of dirt that prevents surface water from flooding the burrow and also serves as a raised platform from which the prairie dog can survey its surroundings and spot potential danger. These circular mounds are conscientiously maintained, and after a rainstorm, a prairie dog family can be seen scurrying about, making necessary repairs.

Although individual burrows vary greatly depending upon their location, most have a main tunnel that goes straight down before dividing into two or three lateral branches. The prairie dogs fill these with grasses and use them as nests for their young and as sleeping and eating chambers for the entire group.

Spraying dust, a prairie dog speedily excavates a burrow (left). The long claws that tip each of its four feet make excellent tools for digging and foraging.

A prairie dog transports a mouthful of grasses and weeds to its underground burrow (right). Among the grasses gathered are those immediately surrounding the burrow entrance, clearing the area of hiding places for enemies.

Home on and off The Range

Against the background of the prairie, the coyote seems as natural as the waving grass and the occasional lone cottonwood. Indeed it was once found only on the plains of western North America, but the coyote has in recent years extended its territory. For years the animal was heavily hunted by farmers who, despite studies to the contrary, were convinced they were losing sheep to the little canine. Perhaps in response to this persecution the intelligent and adaptable coyote began to roam, and today ranges as far north as Alaska, as far south as Central America, and east to Maine and New York.

Tolerant and resourceful, the coyote has been highly successful in adjusting to these diverse habitats. Though its diet consists primarily of rabbits and rodents, the coyote will feast on just about any small animal, including lizards and birds—as well as on cultivated vegetable crops and on the contents of garbage pails.

A pair of coyotes nestle in the prairie underbrush (above). It is thought that coyotes mate for life, and both male and female share the responsibility of rearing their young. When hunting, however, coyotes usually travel alone, like the curious young coyote shown at left approaching a bold prairie dog. Since coyotes themselves are relatively small animals—an adult grows to about three feet long and weighs about 25 pounds—they do not require large quantities of food and the animals they prey on are also small. But when a larger quarry is involved, small family groups are known to work cooperatively to bring it down.

49

Grasslands Underground

Peers of the prairie dog (pages 42–47) as underground burrowers are the badger (below and opposite, bottom) and the black-footed ferret (opposite, top). Both have adopted underground habitats partly as a consequence of their predatory pursuit of prairie dogs. Other burrowers, like the cottontail rabbit and the ground squirrel shown on the following pages, are essentially nonpredatory, using their burrows as bases from which to foray in search of seeds, grasses and nuts. Occasionally mice, insects and birds are included in the ground squirrel's diet.

Like prairie dogs, badgers have been persecuted for decades by ranchers whose horses and cattle sometimes break their legs in badger holes, which may be as deep as 30 feet.

But perhaps because of their varied diet, which, in addition to prairie dogs, includes gophers, marmots and other rodents, badgers have survived.

Black-footed ferrets have not been so lucky. Since these slim-bodied weasels are thought to subsist almost entirely on a diet of prairie dogs, whose burrows they also use for shelter, the ferret population was gravely affected when the dog towns were virtually wiped out by settlers. But while the prairie dog staged a successful comeback elsewhere, the ferret, for reasons yet unexplained, was unable to do so. Today they are exceedingly rare; the black-footed ferret population in South Dakota, for example, is estimated at only 100 animals or fewer.

Chest-deep in its burrow, a black-footed ferret (left) cautiously peers across the landscape. Because they are shy, solitary, nocturnal animals and because there are so few of them left to study, little is known about these creatures with the masklike face markings.

A badger (opposite) waits patiently for the right moment to attack its prey; its flattened, ground-hugging body permits it to go virtually undetected even in the open flatlands. After a successful assault on a prairie dog, the badger drags the carcass (below) off to a burrow, where the predator will stay as long as the food holds out.

A cottontail rabbit (opposite) rests in the shelter of dense underbrush. Of about 13 species of cottontails, only the little Idaho rabbit digs its own burrow. The rest occupy burrows abandoned by other animals. Nocturnal animals, cottontails establish small territories across which they move on definite trails.

Balanced on its short hind legs, a 13-lined ground squirrel (right) pauses during feeding. This squirrel is well adapted to life on the ground, nesting and taking refuge in burrows it either finds or digs for itself. Ground squirrels are diurnal, feeding on low-growing plants, mice, insects and nuts, which they carry in their cheek pouches and store in their burrows.

Mule deer stand on a grassy ridge against a background of
rugged hills of the Great Wall in Badlands National
Monument. Unlike most species of deer found in the Old
World, mule deer are not herd animals, preferring to
travel singly or in pairs. Only when the snow is deep and
food is scarce are groups found foraging together.

The antlers of a mule deer (right) extend from its head like a pair of outstretched hands. These marvelous flowing branches are shed each year between January and March and a new set begins growing around April. Mule deer do not attain a full set of antlers until they are about four or five years old.

Antlered Recluses

Mule deer proliferate in the North American grasslands because there they can find the wide variety of vegetation that makes up their diet. The range of the mule deer extends far beyond the Great Plains—from the Canadian Northwest to northern Mexico. Although they have adapted to widely varying habitats, mule deer generally favor areas with dense vegetation in which they can conceal themselves.

The mule deer, so named for its mulelike ears, is a relative of the white-tailed deer and resembles it closely, with its brownish-gray coat that develops a reddish hue in the summer. But while the whitetail runs with extreme grace, its tail raised to expose its white underside, the mule deer moves in awkward leaps with its tail close to its body.

55

Why the Bear Waddles When He Walks

A Comanche Tale

The approximately 3,000 Comanche Indians who live on privately owned land in Oklahoma once numbered an estimated 25,000, and their nation extended across the American plains from Wyoming to Texas. They shared this land with numerous species of animals, which, like other Indian tribes, they incorporated into their lore and legend. The Comanches were unique among the Plains Indians in their regard for the bear, among the most formidable of their animal neighbors. While the Kiowas feared the bear so much that they would not say the word and the Cheyennes thought themselves descendants of the bear, the Comanches seemed to regard the animal with neither awe nor reverence. This attitude is clearly illustrated in the following Comanche tale. The hand game that is being played is similar to button, button, who's got the button, which was played in some form by North American Indians.

In the beginning days, nobody knew what to do with the sun. It would come up and shine for a long time. Then it would go away for a long time, and everything would be dark.

The daytime animals naturally wanted the sun to shine all the time, so they could live their lives without being interrupted by the dark. The nighttime animals wanted the sun to go away forever, so they could live the way they wanted to.

At last they all got together, to talk things over.

Old Man Coyote said, "Let's see what we can do about that sun. One of us ought to have it, or the other side ought to get rid of it."

"How will we do that?" Scissor-tailed Flycatcher asked. "Nobody can tell the sun what to do. He's more powerful than anyone else in the world."

"Why don't we play a hand game for it?" Bear asked. "The winning side can keep the sun or throw it away, depending on who wins and what they want to do with it."

So they got out the guessing bones to hide in their hands, and they got out the crow-feathered wands for the guessers to point with, and they got out the twenty painted dogwood sticks for the umpires to keep score with. Coyote was the umpire for the day side, and nighttime umpire was Owl.

The umpires got a flat rock, like a table, and laid out their counting sticks on that. Then the two teams brought logs, and lined them up facing one another, with the umpires and their flat rock at one end, between the two teams.

That was a long hand game. The day side held the bones first, and they were so quick and skillful passing them from hand to hand behind their backs and waving them in the guessers' faces that it seemed surely they must win. Then Mole, who was guessing for the night side, caught both Scissor-tail and Hawk at the same time, and the bones went to the night side, and the day people began to guess.

Time and again the luck went back and forth, each team seeming to be about to beat the other. Time and again the luck changed, and the winning team became the losing one.

The game went on and on. Finally the sun, waiting on the other side of the world to find out what was going to happen to him, got tired of it all.

The game was so long that Bear got tired, too. He was playing on the night side. He got cramped sitting on the log, and his legs began to ache. Bear took off his moccasins to rest his feet, and still the game went on and on.

At last the sun was so bored that he decided to go and see for himself what was happening. He yawned and stretched and crawled out of his bed on the underneath side of the world. He started to climb up his notched log ladder to the top side, to find out what was happening.

As the sun climbed the light grew stronger, and the night people began to be afraid. The game was still even; nobody had won. But the sun was coming and coming, and the night animals had to run away. Bear jumped up in such a hurry that he put his right foot in his left moccasin, and his left foot in his right moccasin.

The sun was full up now, and all the other night animals were gone. Bear went after them as fast as he could in his wrong moccasins, rocking and waddling from side to side,

and shouting, "Wait for me! Wait for me!"

But nobody stopped or waited, and Bear had to go waddling along, just the way he has done ever since.

And because nobody won the game, the day and night took turns from that time on. Everybody had the same time to come out and live his life the way he wanted to as everybody else.

Reprieved: A National Icon

The original range of the American bison (popularly and erroneously called the buffalo) extended across almost the entire continent. Sixty million of these majestic animals, the largest land mammals in North America, once roamed the prairies and forests. But it took man only about 70 years to reduce the species nearly to extinction. The destruction of the bison began around 1830 as a means of driving the Indians from their land by killing off their food supply. The slaughter escalated in the 1860s, and near the end of the century, fewer than 300 bison roamed North America.

It was not until approximately 20 bison were left—hidden in the remote recesses of Yellowstone National Park—that Congress acted. In 1894 it passed a law making it illegal to hunt bison in the park. In 1908 the National Bison Range was established in Montana, an example followed soon thereafter by the creation of reserves and national parks in both the United States and Canada. Since then the number of bison has slowly but steadily increased; in 1972 their total population in North America numbered from about 30,000 to 35,000.

In Yellowstone National Park (opposite) a bison grazes on dried grass under snow, which also dapples the shaggy coat of a fellow bison (above) in Wind Cave National Park, South Dakota.

Bison graze in the shadow of jagged cliffs in Badlands National Monument in southwest South Dakota (overleaf). With sweeping motions of their heads, bison can dig through three feet of snow to uncover buried grass and moss.

Patagonia

When Charles Darwin set out on his famous voyage aboard H.M.S. *Beagle* in 1831, one of his chief objectives was to study the wildlife of Patagonia—a remote desert region of South America. Patagonia hardly seemed worthy of the great naturalist's attention, and even today it is a harsh and uninviting land. Bound on the east by the Atlantic and on the west by the Andes, Patagonia is an arid, wind-whipped plateau that constitutes most of the long, narrow cone of land at the southern part of South America. About 400 miles south of Buenos Aires, the fertile pampas end and Patagonia begins, stretching for 1,000 miles to icy Tierra del Fuego at the continent's subantarctic tip.

Dominated by cool, dry air that comes over the mountains from the Pacific and keeps out the Atlantic's moister atmosphere, the climate is severe and usually unpredictable. The dry, yellow soil, which is studded with pebbles, supports only thorny shrubs and clumps of wiry grass, and vegetation is scant even near the ocean and near the scattering of rivers and ponds. Yet Darwin was intrigued by the unique and varied wildlife that had adjusted to this harsh terrain. He was especially fascinated by the guanaco—the domesticated llama's wild relation. This adaptable animal, which once ranged widely over the temperate parts of South America, seemed to thrive in a desert setting, much like its cousin the camel, and Darwin reported seeing a herd of more than 500. There were also large flocks of rheas —the big flightless birds that closely resemble ostriches. The species peculiar to Patagonia is called Darwin's rhea because the naturalist was the first to identify and catalogue it. Among the many rodents that had adapted to the hostile environment was the unique Patagonian cavy, or mara—not to be confused with the desert cavy (right), as the guinea pig is called when it lives in the wild. The giant Patagonian ground sloth also inhabited the region. Identified by fresh remains found in 1898, it was apparently killed off by Tehuelche Indians, the area's only indigenous human inhabitants.

The dusty plateau covering most of the region was also home to an assortment of armadillos, snakes, lizards and birds, and the wooded slopes of the Andes supported cougars and tiny mouse-size opossums as well as two species of native deer—the huemul and the pudu, a miniature creature that stands only a little over a foot high. With the plankton-rich Falkland current sweeping along the Atlantic coastline, shore life was unusually rich. Sea lions, elephant seals and penguins bred and raised their young over long stretches of the bleak coast, while right whales maintained a nursery offshore.

It was the bountiful life along the Patagonian shore that first attracted hunters, who started coming even before Darwin's visit. The large populations of whales, seals and sea lions were reduced to shipload after shipload of hides and oil. Even penguins were caught and boiled for their oil. After Argentina conquered the region in the 1870s and subjugated the Tehuelche Indians, the carnage moved inland, where the rhea was the hardest hit.

Although there was no sudden end to the slaughter, significant changes began at the end of the 19th century, when the altered needs of man combined with the depleted supply of animals to make commercial hunting unprofitable. Nearly all of Patagonia's wildlife has flourished in the last three quarters of a century, though some scars remain. Guanaco herds are not as large or as common as they once were; Darwin's rhea is extinct in many districts; and in some places, rabbits introduced by Europeans have supplanted the native Patagonian cavy. But offsetting these losses is the recovery of the penguins, which are probably more numerous than they were two centuries ago.

With nearly all of the quarter million square miles of Patagonia forming a vast natural refuge, the Argentine government has until now established most of its national parks in the scenic far western Andean parts of the region. At the nation's largest and most popular reserve area, the adjoining Lanin and Naheul Hauapi national parks, guanaco, huemul and pudu—along with the cougars that stalk them—find haven amid a breathtaking landscape of deep lakes, white-capped mountains and extinct volcanos. Most of the same animals are protected in the region's other national parks, including the subantarctic Los Glaciares National Park, where the great glaciers from which the park takes its name hang on the sides of peaks overlooking fjordlike lakes.

The rest of Patagonia, however, will not be protected forever by its remoteness and ruggedness. Increasing human intrusion into the region seems inevitable. Although provinces have started to create some additional refuges, especially along the shore, Argentina's central government has yet to rise to the challenge, and today, even after an unprecedented rebirth, Patagonia's unique wildlife still faces an uncertain future.

Desert cavies

Avian Desert Dwellers

Patagonian bird life is diverse, considering that the sweeping grasslands are almost treeless and afford little or no conventional cover. Flocks of flightless Darwin's rheas (above)—often called South American ostriches—stride across the windy pampas, using their wings to catch the wind and to make sudden shifts in direction. Rheas compensate for their flightlessness by running fast enough to outdistance the fleetest pursuers and with enough agility to outwit less artful predators—quite a feat for 50- to 90-

pound birds that often grow to heights of four or five feet. The cock mates with five or six hens and scrapes out a shallow nest on the desert floor; his harem lays the eggs haphazardly nearby. He gathers the eggs, incubates the clutch for several weeks and assumes complete responsibility for the offspring.

The tawny-throated dotterel (opposite, top) and the southern lapwing (opposite, bottom) are members of the plover family that have adapted to life on the dry plains.

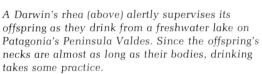

A Darwin's rhea (above) alertly supervises its offspring as they drink from a freshwater lake on Patagonia's Peninsula Valdes. Since the offspring's necks are almost as long as their bodies, drinking takes some practice.

A brooding tawny-throated dotterel (top right) stares dead ahead and counts on a camouflage of pebbly sand to make its nest indistinguishable from the sandy desert.

The southern lapwing at right stalks toward tall grass on the long legs typical of the plover family, while displaying a wary red eye and an elegant crest.

Idle Days in Patagonia

by W. H. Hudson

William Henry Hudson was born in 1851 to an American family living in Argentina. A heart condition that developed during his childhood forced Hudson to live placidly; he spent much of his early life roaming the pampas, where he developed an intense love of and interest in nature that is reflected in his later writings. The following passage from Idle Days in Patagonia *captures the desolate grandeur of this little-known area.*

I spent the greater part of one winter at a point on the Rio Negro, seventy or eighty miles from the sea, where the valley on my side of the water was about five miles wide. The valley alone was habitable, where there was water for man and beast, and a thin soil producing grass and grain; it is perfectly level, and ends abruptly at the foot of the bank or terrace-like formation of the higher barren plateau. It was my custom to go out every morning on horseback with my gun, and, followed by one dog, to ride away from the valley; and no sooner would I climb the terrace and plunge into the grey universal thicket, than I would find myself as completely alone and cut off from all sight and sound of human occupancy as if five hundred instead of only five miles separated me from the hidden green valley and river. So wild and solitary and remote seemed that grey waste, stretching away into infinitude, a waste untrodden by man, and where the wild animals are so few that they have made no discoverable path in the wilderness of thorns. There I might have dropped down and died, and my flesh been devoured by birds, and my bones bleached white in sun and wind, and no person would have found them, and it would have been forgotten that one had ridden forth in the morning and had not returned. Or if, like the few wild animals there—puma, huanaco, and hare-like dolichotis, or Darwin's rhea and the crested tinamou among the birds—I had been able to exist without water, I might have made myself a hermitage of brushwood or dug-out in the side of a cliff, and dwelt there until I had grown grey as the stones and trees around me, and no human foot would have stumbled on my hiding-place.

Not once, nor twice, nor thrice, but day after day I returned to this solitude, going to it in the morning as if to attend a festival, and leaving it only when hunger and thirst and the westering sun compelled me. And yet I had no object in going—no motive which could be put into words; for although I carried a gun, there was nothing to shoot—the shooting was all left behind in the valley. Sometimes a dolichotis, starting up at my approach, flashed for one moment on my sight, to vanish the next moment in the continuous thicket; or a covey of tinamous sprang rocket-like into the air, and fled away with long wailing notes and loud whirr of wings; or on some distant hillside a bright patch of yellow, of a deer that was watching me, appeared and remained motionless for two or three minutes. But the animals were few, and sometimes I would pass an entire day without seeing one animal, and perhaps not more than a dozen birds of any size. The weather at that time was cheerless, generally with a grey film of cloud spread over the sky, and a bleak wind, often cold enough to make my bridle hand feel quite numb. Moreover, it was not possible to enjoy a canter; the bushes grew so close together that it was as much as one could do to pass through at a walk without brushing against them; and at this slow pace, which would have seemed intolerable in other circumstances, I would ride about for hours at a stretch. In the scene itself there was nothing to delight the eye. Everywhere through the light-grey mould, grey as ashes and formed by the ashes of myriads of generations of dead trees, where the wind had blown on it, or the rain had washed it away, the underlying yellow sand appeared, and the old ocean-polished pebbles, dull red, and grey, and green, and yellow. On arriving at a hill, I would slowly ride to its summit, and stand there to survey the prospect. On every side it stretched away in great undulations; but the undulations were wild and irregular; the hills were rounded and cone-shaped, they were solitary and in groups

and ranges; some sloped gently, others were ridge-like and stretched away in league-long terraces, with other terraces beyond; and all alike were clothed in the grey everlasting thorny vegetation. How grey it all was! hardly less so near at hand than on the haze-wrapped horizon, where the hills were dim and outline blurred by distance. Sometimes I would see the large eagle-like, white-breasted buzzard, *Buteo erythronotus,* perched on the summit of a bush half a mile away; and so long as it would continue stationed motionless before me my eyes would remain involuntarily fixed on it, just as one keeps his eyes on a bright light shining in the gloom; for the whiteness of the hawk seemed to exercise a fascinating power on the vision, so surpassingly bright was it by contrast in the midst of that universal unrelieved greyness. Descending from my look-out, I would take up my aimless wanderings again, and visit other elevations to gaze on the same landscape from another point; and so on for hours, and at noon I would dismount and sit or lie on my folded poncho for an hour or longer. One day, in these rambles, I discovered a small grove composed of twenty to thirty trees, about eighteen feet high, and taller than the surrounding trees. They were growing at a convenient distance apart, and had evidently been resorted to by a herd of deer or other wild animals for a very long time, for the boles were polished to a glassy smoothness with much rubbing, and the ground beneath was trodden to a floor of clean, loose yellow sand. This grove was on a hill differing in shape from other hills in its neighbourhood, so that it was easy for me to find it on other occasions; and after a time I made a point of finding and using it as a resting-place every day at noon. I did not ask myself why I made choice of that one spot, sometimes going miles out of my way to sit there, instead of sitting down under any one of the millions of trees and bushes covering the country, on any other hillside. I thought nothing at all about it, but acted unconsciously; only afterwards, when revolving the subject it seemed to me that after having rested there once, each time I wished to rest again the wish came associated with the image of that particular clump of trees, with polished stems and clean bed of sand beneath; and in a short time I formed a habit of returning, animal-like, to repose at that same spot.

Foxes at the Seashore

In Patagonia's Chubut province, on the South Atlantic shoreline, wildlife refuges harbor a diversity of animal life, including the sly, wild Patagonian gray foxes. The gray fox is a handsome, smoky-colored specimen with reddish-brown leg and flank coloration and a bushy, elegant tail tipped with a characteristic black spot.

A heavy, dense coat affords excellent insulation during the fox's winter hunting forays into the ranges of the western Andes or in the forests of Tierra del Fuego. However, the rich, glossy pelts are highly prized by hunters, who are the fox's chief enemy.

The wary creatures have evolved basically nocturnal hunting patterns, sheltering during the day in rocky, well-camouflaged dens or screened from view beneath tree canopies in forested areas. Omnivorous, they venture out to hunt rodents, rabbits, frogs and lizards, and during the autumn months they nibble on the seasonal *pequillin* berry. The foxes occasionally prey upon domestic sheep that have been weakened by disease or are injured and helpless, but do not ordinarily attack healthy livestock.

70

A gray fox runs up the beach displaying its morning's catch, a brown-hooded gull. It will carry its victim into the cover of low bushes fringing the shore before settling down to eat. Ordinarily, gulls are safe on the open beach and avoid the scrub, which offers foxes places to lie in ambush.

A desert cavy (top) examines a shrub before nibbling the leaves. Tiny, tailless rodents, these animals are usually gentle, unaggressive and affectionate—as demonstrated by the pair shown above.

An infant Patagonian cavy (opposite) nurses while its mother keeps watch. (Both are tagged for observation.) Born well developed and ready to walk, the young are alert miniature versions of adults.

Odd Namesakes

Two dissimilar but closely related Patagonian mammals share the name cavy. The nimble, gentle Patagonian cavy, or mara, shown above, with its soft eyes and long, slender legs, bears more visual resemblance to a rabbit than to the desert cavies pictured opposite. Indigenous to the extremely arid Patagonian pampas, the mara often lives among shore-dwelling penguins (overleaf). The mara survives on moisture extracted from the sparse vegetation and burrows deep into the parched, dry soil to make nests for bearing and nurturing offspring. Groups of 40 or more occasionally range single file across the grassy steppes, performing an intricate maneuver called stotting: Each leaps up and tucks all four legs beneath its body as it jumps forward, beginning a series of bounding hops. The mara's sturdy, powerful hind legs are well suited to this bouncing form of locomotion.

73

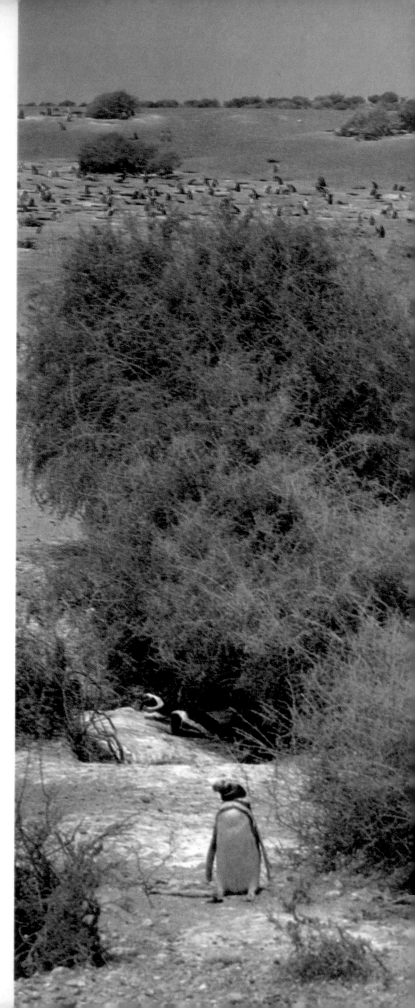

With the so-called stotting motion characteristic of maras (above), one of the energetic little rodents performs a series of running leaps, easily clearing the abandoned penguin burrows that dot the barren landscape of Punta Tumbo. A mara (opposite) settles down to nurse her baby in the midst of a colony of penguins.

Camargue and Coto Doñana

For anyone who has seen the harshly eroded terrain of southern Europe, with its scant growth of stunted brush and evergreens, it is hard to believe that the region was once a semitropical Eden. Yet, before the expanding empires of Greece and Rome cleared the land for wood to build ships and for open acreage to grow food, it was thickly covered with a rich mixture of vegetation where wildcats and lynx stalked deer, ibex and wild sheep. Today, of the vestiges of this wilderness that remain, the most outstanding are in the marshy deltas of two great rivers—the Coto Doñana on the Guadalquivir in Spain and the Camargue on the Rhône in France.

The more pristine of the two is the Coto Doñana, which was protected for centuries as one of the favorite *cotos*, or hunting grounds, of Iberia's nobility and is still the largest area in southern Europe unmarked by roads. It lies about 50 miles downstream from Seville, just northwest of the point where Spain lies closest to Africa.

Doñana is actually a part of a larger region known as Las Marismas, or the marshes. These vast swampy stretches are created by the waters of the Guadalquivir, which meanders over the flat coastal land. These marshlands are constantly changing, following the rhythm of the seasons. Fed by heavy rains in autumn, the river swells and floods most of the region, turning some of the marshes into shallow freshwater lakes. In winter, which is always mild, the Atlantic pushes in and makes many of the wetlands brackish; in spring the melting snows of the Sierra Morena bring a return of fresh water. But as spring progresses the water ebbs, giving way to fields of luxuriant grass, and during the hot, long summer, the land dries into a sunbaked plain. Present in this ever changing scene are a wealth of animals, especially birds. From October through May, the marshes are an avian paradise filled mostly with ducks, greylag geese, flamingos and other waterfowl that pause there on their migratory flights or stay to winter.

Although wetlands predominate, the region is checkered with other kinds of topography, such as woods and plains, which offer shelter to a rich variety of wildlife, including most of Doñana's many mammals. Forests of umbrella pines and ample scrublands that are dotted with ancient cork oaks teem with wild boars, hares, hedgehogs, red and fallow deer, shrews, mongooses and foxes, as well as polecats and wildcats. These sections are also the homes of the two undisputed lords of the Doñana, the scarce pardel lynx and the almost extinct imperial eagle.

Southern Europe's other watery wilderness, the Camargue region of France, is a triangular-shaped island formed by the forking arms of the Rhône as it flows toward the Mediterranean. A short drive from Marseilles, France's second largest city, the Camargue shows more signs of man's intrusions than Spain's remote delta. Vineyards, rice and asparagus fields cover much of the northern Camargue, and throughout the neighboring region there is a sprinkling of villages, most dating back to medieval times. But protected by its limited access, most of the area has remained truly wild. It is a land always being shaped and changed by the sluggish waters of the streams and rivers and the pounding tides of the Mediterranean.

Although the Camargue seems to be much more of an unrelieved marshland than Coto Doñana, it too has amid its marshes a diverse mix of other terrain, including brambly heaths, grassy meadows and forests along the rivers at its edges. In the center lies an extensive but shallow lagoon punctuated with wooded islands. Like the Coto Doñana, the Camargue is subject to seasonal oscillations between flood and drought, but they occur in a climate of greater extremes. Winters are harsher—the lagoons often freeze over, and the mistral, a cold, wet wind originating in the Alps, may blow for a week at any time of year.

Waterfowl are the glory of the Camargue. Ducks, gulls, terns and herons are among the most numerous. But the most spectacular are the great colonies of flamingos, which have made this patch of coast their only regular breeding ground in Europe. A large number of mammals also find refuge here, including hares, badgers, wild boars, martens, weasels, foxes and the continent's smallest furry creature, the Etruscan shrew, which measures less than two inches. The most famous inhabitants of the Camargue, however, are its semiwild horses, snowy-coated equines that seem almost aquatic in this marshland and are usually glimpsed splashing through the ponds and lagoons.

A large tract in the center of the Camargue was set aside in 1928 as a strictly limited-access preserve. After being maintained for decades by concerned individuals, the Coto Doñana and adjoining parts of Las Marismas were bought by the World Wildlife Fund in 1969 and presented to the Spanish government. Now, with their survival assured, these enclaves of marshy wilderness shine like jewels in the man-transformed landscape of southern Europe.

Purple gallinule

Uneasy Coexistence

The 179 species of birds that nest in the marshlands and on the colossal, great-armed cork oaks of the Coto Doñana constitute most of this sanctuary's vertebrate animal population. There is keen competition among the larger birds for nest sites in the great oak trees. Since the sites are limited, members of several species rarely found together outside the sanctuary noisily coexist. Imperial eagles and storks build their enormous homes in the tops of trees; spoonbills, herons, magpies, kites and other birds congregate on the lower branches. Although this suggests domination of the smaller birds by the larger, curiously, each bird nests in precisely the same location it ordinarily favors. The different species guard their enclaves vigorously, but occasionally a bird will steal twigs from a nearby nest while the adult birds are away.

A squacco heron (top left) snatches a fish out of one of the many pools that dot its marshland home. Nearby, a pratincole on the lookout for insects (left) stands in marshy shallows.

A group of spoonbills and grey herons (above) perches in a tall cork oak tree. Large flocks of spoonbills often take over an entire tree, whitewashing the trunk and branches with their droppings.

A pair of black kites (left) gaze out over the marshland of the Coto Doñana, searching for something to eat. Kites will feed on fish, amphibians, insects and reptiles—even the poisonous viper—and also prey on heron chicks, which they snatch from the nest while the parents are away.

A griffon vulture and one of its young settle down on their nest (left). These vultures usually group on ledges in the Andalusian mountains, which border the Coto Doñana preserve. The birds leave their nests and soar over the preserve for hours, looking for dead or weakened animals to eat.

An imperial eagle stands guard over a maturing nestling (right). Ornithologists fear that this Spanish subspecies will be extinct within 50 years. Of the two or three eggs produced by each pair every year, barely one chick will survive, and young birds that fly out of the preserve are impossible to protect from killing by human hunters.

Airborne Hunters

The Coto Doñana has one of Europe's largest concentrations of birds of prey. Vultures and buzzards constantly circle overhead scouting for food, and clouds of spiraling black kites, the enemies of the park's heron population, are breathtaking in their gyrations. But the undisputed king of the air in Coto Doñana is the Spanish imperial eagle.

Centuries ago the imperial eagle was common throughout the Iberian Peninsula, but now is rarely seen beyond the borders of the Coto Doñana. These eagles need to estab-lish enormous territories for themselves, and Doñana's 12 pairs are as many as its 27 square miles can support. Imperial eagles are excellent hunters. They can remain in the air for hours and then, when they have spotted prey, will dive down almost vertically, moving so fast that they make a humming noise. The flamingo, a prey of the eagle, is so terrified of an attack that if threatened, it panics, closes its wings in flight and falls to the earth—killing itself before the eagle gets near.

A lynx of Spain's Coto Doñana (left) rests after a meal—probably a rabbit, one of its favorite foods. Lynx will also hunt deer, and have been known to catch partridge in midair with their strong, sharp-clawed forepaws.

On the prowl for something to eat, a lynx moves about noiselessly on thickly furred feet (below). The lynx of the sanctuary are usually nocturnal animals, but on chilly days they will leave their lairs to lie in the sun or go hunting.

A Spotted King

If the imperial eagle (pages 80–81) epitomizes the denizens of the air in the Coto Doñana, the pardel lynx represents the region's land inhabitants as does no other animal. Lynx originally roamed over most wooded areas of southern Europe. Now, after centuries of being hunted as a predator-pest, they are indigenous only to certain areas of eastern Europe and the Iberian Peninsula. Legends about the lynx have portrayed it as an evil animal—one that kills just for the sake of killing—and such stories have contributed to its virtual extinction. But today the Coto Doñana provides safe sanctuary for the scarce lynx population.

Along with many birds of the Coto Doñana, the lynx often makes its home in the enormous cork oak tree. With age the tree sometimes becomes hollow, and the lynx simply finds a suitable tree with a comfortable hole and climbs inside. At times, a lynx will take over a stork's nest.

Haven for Horses

Between the branches of the Rhône, south of Arles along the Mediterranean, lies one of the most untouched regions of Europe, the 26,000-acre Camargue nature reserve: a wild and watery patchwork of salt lagoons, freshwater ponds, sandy beaches, flooded meadows and, where the land rises a significant few inches above sea level, patches of drier grassland and heath. This isolated, eerie land is the home of half-wild horses whose mysterious origins have been a source of fascination for centuries. Known to experts as grays, the adults appear white, with dark areas on legs and muzzles.

Though some authorities say that they are descended from the wild horses of Mongolia, these stocky, sturdy animals almost certainly had semidomesticated European ancestors, and thus cannot be classified as a true wild species. Nevertheless, in 1968 they were formally classified by the French as a separate equine breed. Members of this exclusive band live for the most part without any helping hand from man, moving together surefootedly across the marshy ground, grazing on the limited supplies of dry vegetation and joyfully plunging deep into ponds to gorge on aquatic plants. The horses seem to thrive on their self-sufficiency. They often live for more than 20 years and a hardy old age of 30 is not uncommon. In a record of their numbers that dates back to 1550, the latest count of mares is 750, and each will bear up to 20 foals in her lifetime. It is estimated that if their rare habitat is preserved, the extraordinary herds are sure to increase.

A family herd of mares, foals and a stallion grazes across a rare swath of high ground in the Camargue. The color of their coats is a key to their ages: The foals are born with coats of dark brown or black; as the horses mature, their coats become paler until, at four or five years old, they appear nearly pure white, as is typical of their breed. Some horses, including the stallion in the lead, have been branded for identification.

Master of Mares

The spontaneous existence of the Camargue horses is disrupted by man in one crucial aspect: Local ranchers select the stallion that will lead each herd and breed with its mares, and they cull from the herds the three- to four-year-old stallions that, under natural conditions, would count as competition for the dominant male. For a time these young stallions live together apart from any herd and, following their instinct to dominate, their lives are a constant rearing round of kicks and bites that are more playful practice than serious combat. Most of these young bloods will be gelded and become agile and lively saddle horses for the local tourist trade.

For the chosen stallion that heads a harem—an average of 18 mares—life can be strenuous, especially in the May mating season when his skittish mares may be shy and indifferent or demanding and aggressive. Yet they are totally dependent on his authority, and if at any time he is absent, they become lost and confused.

A group of young water-loving Camargue horses (left) gathers on a sandy beach at the edge of the Mediterranean. Two- to four-year-old horses often wander together in their own leaderless, free-spirited herds.

A young stallion (above), ears laid back in anger and teeth bared, stretches his neck to nip a rival. Instinctive competition leads to constant sparring among young males, but the result of a battle is usually a draw.

Safety in Speed and Spines

For some of the smaller species of mammals that live in the Camargue, the region is a perfect place. The hedgehog and the European hare, for example, are both prolific and hardy creatures that never build a burrow, although the hedgehog, a hibernating insectivore, may use an old rabbit hole in which to bear its young or to spend the winter. Both animals are solitary and nocturnal, and find abundant food in the meadows and scrub woodlands. The hare feeds on grasses and shrubs; the slow-moving hedgehog is happy on a diet of slugs, snails and worms. Living without much cover is not particularly dangerous for these two: The hare can run with exceptional speed and the hedgehog has the ability to curl up into a nearly impregnable, spine-covered ball. The hunter's gun is the hare's worst enemy, and the hedgehog, an inveterate wanderer on roads, is threatened mainly by the automobile.

With long-legged leaps, a European brown hare (left) heads for tall grass to elude a pursuer. For this fleet-footed hare, outdistancing most predators is no problem: In short bursts it can attain speeds of up to 50 miles per hour.

A normally nocturnal hedgehog takes a daytime dip (above). The nine-inch animal is adept at swimming, especially when chased by one of the few local creatures not put off by its spines—a fox, badger or wild boar.

A purple heron (left) patrols the edges of a reedy lagoon, looking for the small fishes that it feeds on. This two-and-a-half-foot-tall bird has relatively short legs for a heron, but its boldly marked neck is longer than most and its feet are specially adapted for perching on the stalks of reeds.

A pair of young long-eared owls (below) attempt to intimidate an intruder. Not as expert in defense as they will be when they are 14-inch adults, these juveniles react to danger with a threatening display, fluffing out their feathers so they will appear larger, and hissing and snapping their beaks in an act that is basically bluff.

Luxury Bird Resort

The 138,000 acres of the Camargue delta are a lap of luxury for many of France's 400 species of birds, providing a wealth of habitats that are not only watery but also wooded. The banks of the rivers are lined with galleries of woods; groves of trees and thickets of tamarisk stand in the wild meadows; and even the cultivated fields have rows of hedges and lines of cypress and poplar that have been planted as windbreaks.

The long-eared owls and purple heron shown here require vastly different habitats: The purple heron thrives in lagoons or ditches that are densely packed with reeds, while the arboreal long-eared owl prefers the drier upland reaches with copses of conifers in which to nest or hide during the day. The long-eared owl is distinguished by the closely set ear tufts above its golden-yellow eyes, and it is a wide-ranging predator that inhabits Asia and North America as well as Europe. It is an excellent mouser at any time of year, hunting nocturnally in open country, but in breeding season it also feeds on small birds. Southern France is warm enough for long-eared owls even in the winter, when they often roost together in small groups. But the colonies of purple herons that breed and nest in the reed beds during the spring and summer take off for tropical climates in the fall, flying as far south as central Africa.

Southern Africa

Among its immensely diverse terrains, Africa boasts two of the world's greatest expanses of aridity. The Sahara sprawling across the north is the best known and the one most approaching a total wasteland. But to the south, the continent has another sunbaked zone, consisting of sandy deserts and scrubby semideserts mixed with parched savannas, where grass and bush survive on a scant 10 inches of rainfall a year.

This region is much smaller than its northern counterpart, but it is nonetheless vast—extending over an area more than twice the size of Texas. It takes a healthy bite out of the Republic of South Africa, but it almost completely consumes two adjoining countries: Botswana and Namibia. With well over half of its territory given over to the great Kalahari Desert, the inland nation of Botswana is "thirsty cattle country" in the minds of its inhabitants. And with the harsh Namib Desert stretching for a thousand miles along its Atlantic coastline, Namibia—until recently the territory of South-West Africa—is locally known as "the land made by God in anger."

Before the arrival of Europeans in the 19th century, this inhospitable swath of southern Africa was able to support a surprisingly large and varied collection of animals that survived through the balanced use of meager resources. Antelopes were especially abundant, and they included not only species such as eland and gemsbok, which can exist on little water, but also wildebeest, kudu, steenbok, springbok and impala, which were able to quench their thirst at the scattered water holes. Zebras, elephants and giraffes were also numerous. These herds of large grazers migrated with a natural rhythm across the land, feeding on one scrubby patch after another without ever fully depleting any. Always trailing them were predators and scavengers—lions, leopards, cheetahs, jackals, vultures, buzzards and hyenas.

Man's influence weighed lightly on this delicately balanced scale. The area was only scantly populated, and much of it by Bushmen, (now called San), who did little more than pick off an occasional antelope or giraffe with the aid of a dog pack and an arrow or spear dipped in a disabling toxin brewed from local plants or insects. But after its discovery by Europeans—Namibia was a German colony from 1884 to 1915—the area suffered from many of the same problems as the rest of the continent. The great African explorer David Livingstone noted as early as 1853 that ivory hunters were causing a substantial drop in Botswana's elephant population. Other animals were killed for their hides and still others were shot as pests. Livestock were introduced in much greater numbers, and the destruction they brought was rapid and catastrophic. Around the turn of the century, a severe epidemic of rinderpest —a virulent wasting disorder much like hoof-and-mouth disease—wiped out large numbers of Namibia's wildlife. But, ironically, this disaster was responsible for the great proliferation of wild animals in that country today. The northern part of the territory was hardest hit—a region centering around an ancient lake bottom known as the Etosha Pan. Most of the stock raisers had to flee, and an enlighted German colonial governor took advantage of the exodus to set aside much of the area as a preserve.

Thereafter Namibia's animals made a slow but substantial recovery, and today Etosha Pan National Park is among the largest refuges in Africa, covering 38,000 square miles—an area the size of Indiana. It is also one of the best protected, and enormous herds range over a mixed terrain of deserts, bushlands and the salt flats of the pan itself. Despite its size, some elephants still find the park a bit confining, and among the keepers' biggest problems are the herds that simply push over sections of the 8½-foot, 300-mile fence along the southern border and create havoc in the adjacent settlements. To the south, Namibia maintains another gigantic safe haven for animals, extending over 5,000 square miles of mountains, plains and dunes in the heart of the Namib Desert. Here, the rare Hartmann's mountain zebra is believed to number nearly 10,000.

The Kalahari Gemsbok National Park, in Botswana, is also one of Africa's largest game reserves. Though a scattering of San live and hunt within its boundaries, the protection of animals, especially the large herds of antelopes, has been total since 1931. Most of the nation's other preserves are less secure asylums where hunting for exportable hides is common. In recent years this destruction has been brought under control by licensing and by laws protecting endangered species, and plans now call for greatly increasing the number of refuges in the country.

Even in this barren corner of Africa, the population of people and livestock increases each year, but because of the enormous amount of land that has been set aside, the preservation of wildlife—especially large animals that need vast tracts of open range—has been extremely effective.

Black-maned lion

Tough Cats

The wildlife reserves of southern Africa's Kalahari Desert provide safety and refuge for tens of thousands of animals, including the regal black-maned lion (above) and the svelte cheetah (opposite, top and bottom). But the mostly barren terrain and the harsh weather in which these animals live have forced them to develop special behavioral patterns to survive. The little rainfall the area receives comes in late summer. For their water supply during the rest of the year, the cats must rely on the moisture in desert fruits and rain that has been collected in the scattering of water holes drilled by park rangers.

Not surprisingly, the parched land supports only a few trees and shrubs, leaving little cover for predators when they hunt. The lion may travel as much as 30 miles a night in search of food, and it can go for days without filling its stomach.

The gemsbok, a small, numerous antelope, is the lion's favorite food, but in lean times the lordly feline will subsist on such unlikely game as porcupines, bringing down the thorny creatures with a deft slap on the face. The lion uncovers the flesh of its prickly prey by pulling out the quills with its teeth and claws—a potentially dangerous task for the cat, which can be disabled by infection if just one of the spines becomes lodged in its sensitive paws.

Cheetahs (top) pause on a sandy rise to scan the surrounding terrain. A female cheetah (above), along with her youngster, devours a freshly killed animal. Fastest of the land mammals over short distances, the long-legged cheetahs still find it hard to eke out a living in the Kalahari.

Kalahari Antelopes

The most numerous and most varied group of animals that roam the African continent are the antelopes. Although primarily inhabitants of scrub country and grasslands, these hoofed herbivores also browse and graze in many other habitats, including the sandy plains of southern Africa's Kalahari Desert.

Actually the Kalahari, unlike the Namib Desert to its west, is not a true desert. Many parts of the Kalahari's 100,000-square-mile expanse are covered with a variety of plant life that supports a vast array of animal species, including the lesser kudu (below), the steenbok (opposite) and some of their relatives, which are shown on the following pages.

The Kalahari provides a relatively plentiful source of grasses and water for these animals, although they must often wander great distances to find either. Nevertheless, most species have adapted admirably to these conditions, and some, such as the handsome gemsbok (overleaf), need not drink water for long stretches, obtaining enough moisture from the vegetation they feed on.

The Kalahari's open spaces offer ideal protection for antelopes, which generate their greatest speeds over such obstacle-free terrain. African antelopes are now protected species within the borders of southern Africa's reserves, where zoologists and conservationists have been able to study their feeding habits. Such studies have shown that large and diverse herds of grazing wild animals can live successfully on an area's limited vegetation without destroying their source of food, because they move constantly to new sources and do not destroy the roots of plants.

Large ears raised alertly, a steenbok (right) pauses from feeding on desert plants. These tiny, two-foot-tall antelopes usually live alone, forming pairs only during the breeding season. When danger threatens, steenbok often take shelter underground in such places as the abandoned burrows of other animals.

Female lesser kudus (below) gather around a water hole in southern Africa. The female kudu is smaller than the male and lacks his twisted, spiraling horns. The sides of both sexes, however, bear vertical white markings.

A group of gemsbok (below) rests in a field of scrub brightened with green by seasonal rains. These handsome parti-colored animals survive well under desert conditions and are able to withstand extended periods of drought and variations in their body temperature.

On an open stretch of the Kalahari Desert a herd of springbok (left) stands serene. Once the most numerous antelope in southern Africa, these graceful animals, known for their distinctive leaps, have been intensively hunted for their hides and meat, and are now found only on reserves.

98

Fleeing a predator, a pair of hartebeests (above) bound
across the desert landscape. Hartebeests are normally
trusting and unwary, but they have learned to be quite
cautious in areas close to human settlements: One member
of the herd acts as sentinel while the others graze or rest.

The Lost World of the Kalahari

by Laurens van der Post

The San, or Bushmen, as they were once called, are a people of southern Africa who number about 50,000. While many have left their Kalahari Desert home, thousands of others still lead the traditional life of nomadic hunters. Laurens van der Post, an author and farmer born and raised in South Africa, wrote The Lost World of the Kalahari *as a paean to these remarkable people. The excerpt reprinted below describes the almost spiritual hunt for an eland, an animal whose grace and intelligence have earned it a special place in the San's life and lore.*

One morning, soon after sunrise, we came on the fresh spoor of a herd of about fifty eland. When I saw Nxou's wrists flicking over it as he found it, I had a feeling that our hunter's day had really come. We followed the spoor resolutely all morning into the climax of the day without catching up with the herd. Nxou, Bauxhau, and Txexchi kept hard at it, trotting silently beside the spoor in the scarlet sand. From time to time I joined them but could

not have kept up except for repeated rests in my Land-Rover. About three in the afternoon they drew near enough to have a shot at the herd. I happened to have dropped back at the time to try and persuade a ten-foot mamba with the biggest eyes I had ever seen to pose for the camera, and when I caught up again I found that the herd had gone off so fast into the east that there had been no time to find out whether they had been hit. But from that moment the hunters raced after the great antelope.

I had seen them run many times before, yet never with this reserve of power nor with such length and ease of stride. I am certain they ran as only the Greek who brought the news of Marathon to Athens could have run. Their minds were entirely enclosed in the chase and impervious to fatigue or other claims on their senses. With Ben driving at his best through bush, scrub and over hyena and ant-bear holes, with the Land-Rover momentarily airborne and going over each obstacle like a steeplechaser over a

hurdle, we only just managed to keep close to Nxou, who was in the lead. At one point I was horrified to see a bright yellow and deadly Kalahari cobra uncoiling like a twist of saffron rope from behind a bush and, hood extended, rise swiftly to strike at Nxou. Without a hesitation or swerve he rose like a hurdler high into the air and sailed over the angry head from which a forked tongue, shining with spittle, flickered like lightning. He didn't even look back at the snake but held on straight to the freshening spoor.

From the point where the final chase began to where we caught a glimpse of the full herd again, they ran thus without pause, for twelve miles according to Ben's speedometer. And the final mile was an all-out sprint. So fast did they go on this stretch that they passed momentarily out of our straining vision. We were climbing up a steep dune through a thick matted bush of thorn and the finest and deepest of blood-red sand underneath. Large ant-bear and spring-hare holes pitted the dune like shell holes on a ridge

of modern battle. Superbly as Ben led us in his Land-Rover, we were inevitably slowed down. For the first time I feared the chase would fail. From the smoking tracks of the eland in the sensitive sand and the clearly defined length of stride they recorded on it, it was obvious that the herd was thoroughly alarmed and running full out. Yet they were not over-far ahead: the spoor was so fresh that it glistened darkly in the crumbling sand. That, and the fact that our Bushman hunters had suddenly spurted ahead, alone, checked my fears.

Then suddenly we broke out of the thorn on the crest of the dune, to see Ben and Vyan, guns in hand, tumbling out of their Land-Rover abruptly halted. I drew up sharply, snatched my rifle from Dabe and jumped out to run over to join them. The sun was low and its full light flowing like a broad, flashing stream down an immense dried-up watercourse coming out of the west and going due east. The watercourse was bare of trees and covered with long yellow grass. Immediately below us, running full out as if the race had only just begun, were our hunters, their sweating shoulders copper and gold above the erect grass. And most wonderful of all, half-way up the

bank opposite us was the whole herd of eland purple and silver in the sun and drawn by their fear into one tight motionless ring, staring out of their wide eyes in our direction. Though they were five hundred yards or more from us, it was impossible for people who knew them as well as we did not to read in the angle of their heads and the close formation into which they were formed, their dismay that after so long a chase they should still be pursued.

"They'll be off in a second," Ben cried out in alarm. "Far as it is we'll have to shoot at once if we're to get our Bushmen their meat."

As he spoke, a great bull broke out of the paralytic ring of the herd with an enormous bound high into the air. He might have been a lithe springbuck, instead of a creature weighing nearly a ton, for the ease with which he did it. A spurt of red dust rose in the yellow grass as his feet found the earth and immediately he led off with the speed of a race-horse straight up the side of the dune. So fast did the rest of the herd come out of their huddle and follow on one another's heels in single file that the herd went over the grass-gold dune on the far side like a single twist of silk.

Fastidious hunters that they were, fearful of hitting the eland women and their young, Vyan and Ben fired almost simultaneously at the flying bull, but the distance was great and the target erratic, and though they tried again and again he vanished unscathed over the dune.

I very nearly joined in to fire at the same target but something in me had already marked the fact that our Bushman hunters were not making for the main herd. Excited as I was by seeing the magnificent bull leading his herd out of their trance and the noise of Ben and Vyan opening up on him, I checked my impulse long enough to have another look at our hunters. Then I saw it all: another great bull, nearly two hundred yards behind the main herd, was coming out of the bed of the watercourse on the farthest side. He too, the moment the firing started, bounded forward but much more slowly than the rest of the herd. In one so great and massive as he it could only mean that he was wounded and that despite the length and speed of the chase Nxou and Bauxhau had read his condition accurately from the spoor in the sand and made him their special quarry. Nonetheless, the bull was still going strongly enough to prolong the chase for an hour or more,

since the sun was dangerously low. I shot at him immediately and managed to hit him in the hindquarters. He faltered, walked on holding his head all the higher in the instinctive pride of so noble a breed that it makes the male scorn all sense of physical injury, but he suddenly sank back onto his hindquarters into the grass. Even then he went on holding his head up to look steadily at the little hunters closing in on him with their spears.

Running toward them, gun in hand, as fast as I could go, I still had time to notice how small they looked beside him as they went in spear in hand for the kill. They drove their spears straight at his heart, and when I came up to them Nxou was working his round in the heart of the bull to help him as quickly as possible over the end. But it's a law of life observed devoutly by the great animal kingdom of Africa: that one does not die unless one must. Great as was his pain and hopeless as the cause of life was for him, this lone bull still observed the royal law and would not accept the release of death. So I motioned our Bushman away and put a bullet in his head.

Hardly was he dead than Nxou and Bauxhau started skinning the bull. That was the amazing part of the chase; without pause or break for rest, they were fresh enough at the end to plunge straight away into the formidable task of skinning and cutting up the heavy animal.

As we watched them do it in the closing hour of the day, we noticed an expression on their faces that we had not seen before. Suddenly a deep laugh broke from Nxou. His arms covered with blood, he stood up from his work and said something to Bauxhau, who giggled like an excited girl. Dabe, hearing them, threw the round, shabby little European hat he insisted on wearing high into the air, and in the grip of the same excitement called out in wild approval, "Oh, you child of a Bushman, you!"

I asked him what it all meant.

"Master," he said almost beside himself, "now we are going to dance!"

I turned to Nxou and asked, "Why now?"

Because, he said, with a freedom I had not experienced before, always, ever since the days of the first Bushman, no hunter had ever killed an eland without thanking it with a dance.

Bush Mammals

The meerkat is just one of the many small mammals that inhabit the sandy, gravelly terrain of southernmost Africa, south of the Orange River. Also called suricates, meerkats are rabbit-size creatures very similar to mongooses and, like them, are unselective carnivores that eat insects, mice, small birds and reptiles. Using their well-developed sense of smell to detect their prey, meerkats scrape the ground with their long, strong claws to unearth their victims. Meerkats subdue larger quarry by first striking and holding prey with their forepaws, and then delivering a fatal bite. Some meerkats are especially fond of eating scorpions, but before rending and devouring one, they make sure to bite off the scorpion's extremely poisonous tail at its base.

A newborn meerkat is blind at birth and has closed ears. Both eyes and ears open when the youngster is about two weeks old. Highly sociable animals, they make diligent and attentive parents. Because meerkats can be tamed easily, South Africans make pets of them.

Meerkats catch the warming rays of the morning sun near their den. Several meerkat families may live in a burrow in a colony. To conserve body heat they sleep piled one on top of another.

With their extremely long legs and their necks stretched straight out for balance, flamingos in flight (right) are a spectacular sight. On land the long legs and haughtily held head give the bird an elegant look, and the peculiar curving and angling of its neck while preening or feeding demonstrate its balance and agility.

Flamingo Flyby

The flamingos that live in the Etosha Pan of Namibia manage to survive in the Pan's salt lakes—waters that almost all other animals would reject as uninhabitable. The lakes, however, support a vast amount of algae, the flamingo's primary food in this region. To take in food the flamingo dips its curved beak into the water, and then, lifting its head, uses its bill with its toothlike edges to strain and sift a multitude of tiny food particles.

Since so few animals find the saltwater-lake environment of the flamingo hospitable, virtually no predators menace its newly hatched chicks. The extensive mud flats surrounding the Etosha Pan are an additional barrier that prevents even a determined mammalian predator from getting out to the shallow water where the flamingos feed. Populations of both the lesser and greater flamingo at the Etosha Pan are quite erratic from year to year—fluctuating from a peak of more than one million birds of both species to none at all—and prolific breeding there is more the exception than the rule, since success depends on water supply and direct rainfall.

The Indian Subcontinent

Reverence for life in all forms has been a central tenet of Hinduism for over four millennia. Yet nowhere on the globe is the very survival of wildlife as threatened as it is on Hinduism's home ground, the Indian subcontinent, where the hungry competition of a growing human population is forcing wild creatures toward a tragic retreat.

Only a century ago, the subcontinent was still an enormous reservoir of animal life in habitats as richly varied as any on the face of the earth. On the western coast, dense tropical forests reverberated with the crow of jungle cocks and the babble of monkeys. Farther up the coast and inland, herds of zebra-like wild asses roamed the desert area known as the Little Rann of Kutch, and flocks of wild sheep grazed the mountain pastures of the land now called Pakistan. On the eastern coast crocodiles slithered through the mangrove swamps and reed marshes of the valleys and river deltas. On the great central plateau, the vast stretches of grasslands that ran between stands of deciduous trees were open range for herds of deer and wild cattle as well as for the tigers and other great cats that stalked them. In the far north, alpine plains and the precipitous slopes of the Himalayas were home to wild goats and the beautiful tragopan, an exotic pheasant, while the foothills boasted the unique pygmy hog, a hare-size wild boar.

For India's princely rulers and the imperial British, the country was a sportsman's paradise. One favorite quarry of the shikar, or hunt, was the black buck—prized for its spiral-twisted horns—and men can still remember when giant herds were a common sight on the Indian plains. This diminutive antelope is so swift—able to cover up to 20 feet in a leap—that it was hunted with trained cheetahs. Today the black buck is numerous in only a few preserves, but its fate is far better than that of its pursuer, the cheetah, which may well be extinct in southwest Asia.

The British withdrew with the independence of India and Pakistan in 1947, but the shikar tradition stayed on. However, the carnage inflicted by the gun was minor compared to the more insidious damage of the plow. Forest after forest was felled, first for firewood and lumber, then for the fertile humus that would provide tillage for millions of landless peasants and food for a population that was growing by the equivalent of a new Bombay—six million people—each year. The grassy central plains were quickly carved up for agriculture, as were the tracts of tall ulu grass in the sparsely populated northeast that was home for the once abundant Assam rabbit. And drainage of wet meadowlands almost spelled doom for the Siberian white crane, which once wintered in the Ganges valley but is now found only in the Bharaptpur Bird Sanctuary, and for the swamp deer, which once roamed in prodigious herds.

Little was done to rescue the subcontinent's wildlife until the early 1970s, when the alarm created by the near disappearance of the Indian tiger drew attention to the similar plight of many other species. Since then most countries of the subcontinent have set stiff penalties for the killing of endangered species, and have restricted the export of hides and pets. In India, much has been done to protect and expand the parks and refuges established by the British. Two have been especially successful. At Kanha National Park in the state of Madhya Pradesh on the central plateau, tigers prowl, and herds of swamp deer, black buck and chital, or axis deer, graze alongside sambar stags and gaurs, the Indian bison. Kaziranga National Park, in the eastern province of Assam, is best known as the sanctuary for half of the great Indian one-horned rhinos, but its swampy terrain also shelters an array of wild Asiatic buffalo, jackals, hog deer, wild boars, mongooses, pythons and cobras. In its three national parks, Sri Lanka (formerly called Ceylon) has successfully protected many of the island's unique subspecies, including its elephants.

Most of the region's other preserves are less inviolate as sanctuaries. Legal and illegal hunting, logging and grazing continue in the poorly guarded parks of Pakistan, Bangladesh and Nepal. And not all of India's other refuges are as secure as Kanha and Kaziranga national parks. Bharaptpur Bird Sanctuary, a hundred miles south of New Delhi, is a marshy paradise inhabited by 322 species of birds, 110 of them migratory. But for a small fee a herdsman can still graze his water buffalo in the sanctuary, and birds are frequently netted for the pet trade. Even preserves in the remote foothills of the Himalayas are not immune from the guns of local tribesmen, who kill musk stags for glands that fetch a high price in New Delhi as a cure for impotence.

The outlook for the survival of the subcontinent's precious heritage of wildlife is not as bleak as it was only a very few years ago. But because the human population of an area about one third the size of the United States is expected to swell to well over a billion by the year 2000, the best hope will be to reinforce the region's reserves and create secure islands that can weather an ever threatening sea of people.

Indian one-horned rhinoceros

In the swampy lowlands of Kaziranga, an Indian rhinoceros (left) wallows in one of the region's abundant, secluded mudholes for its daily bathing ritual. Rhinos need a place to take mud baths, which help regulate their body temperature and keep their skin healthy.

Protected Giants

The main refuge of the 700 remaining Indian rhinoceroses is the flat marshland of the Brahmaputra River's southern bank, designated in 1928 as the Kaziranga Wildlife Sanctuary. The rhinos of the Indian subcontinent differ from those of Africa in having only one horn and hairless thick skin creased with folds that gives an illusion of impenetrable armor. Formerly free to roam all along the Ganges river basin, they gradually lost their reed jungle habitat to cropland, and their numbers were further reduced as poachers continued to shoot them for their horns, which were believed to have magical medicinal properties. Growing from the upper surface of the nose, the rhino's horn is composed of keratin, which is akin to the material of fingernails and hair. Less imposing than it looks, the horn is occasionally ripped away from the head in a fight.

A rhino seldom charges, preferring retreat to attack, but when wounded or defending its young, the animal uses its sharp, pointed lower tusks—formidable weapons indeed when backed up by its massive weight of up to four tons.

Rhinos wander near a river in the sanctuary. They feed during the cooler, shadier morning and evening hours and sleep when the temperature rises in the middle of the day. Shy and elusive, they favor remote areas, where they munch on grass, reeds and twigs.

A pair of gharials lie like logs (right), eyes, ears and nostrils well above the waterline. A transparent, protective membrane slides over its eyes when the gharial dives underwater, and flaps make its ears watertight. The nostrils are adapted so that the gharial can breathe even if its mouth is wide open underwater.

A lone gharial lurks near a riverbank, where its burrow is dug just above the waterline and extends for several yards, terminating in a small chamber where prey can be stashed and eaten at leisure.

A Singular Croc

For the Indian gharial (also called gavial), Corbett National Park in the foothills of the Himalayas is a haven where this fast-disappearing link with prehistoric reptiles is strictly protected.

Classified in a separate crocodilian family because of a characteristically slender, narrow snout, the gharial is also the one crocodilian with an external sex differentiation—the male develops a bulbous knob at the tip of its muzzle during the reproductive period.

The gharial is an aggressive feeder, clamping its jaws down with an abrupt, sideways jerk of the snout and overpowering its prey. Rotating its body slowly, the gharial swiftly dismembers the carcass, using its teeth not for chewing, but for grasping the victim firmly. The remains are often dragged back to the gharial's burrow for safekeeping. Like all crocodilians, this one is a loner, establishing territorial boundaries and warning off intruders with an intimidating roar. Tensing its body, vibrating its flanks to splash jets of water high into the air, the gharial underlines its determination to hunt unmolested. These creatures are amphibious, but because of weak legs, the gharial is less at home on land than in water, and uses its powerful tail to propel itself stealthily and efficiently through the currents.

A small barasingha herd (above) includes young hinds, and stags "in velvet"—their antlers covered with downy material that will be rubbed off as the antlers mature. One stag has thrust his antlers into a clump of grass, an aggressive act often observed during the mating season.

Sheltered Natives Of the Swamp

Although the gentle barasinghas, or swamp deer, shown below and left, are protected in several Indian preserves, poaching by local villagers is still a serious threat. However, Kaziranga National Park provides rigid enforcement and adequate protection, with lush, green foliage and ample water ensuring year-round, plentiful sources of nourishment. Swamp deer, covered with firm, water-repellent coarse hair, graze in marshlands, their flexible toes assuring good footing as they venture into the pools where they forage for water plants.

Seeking out the moist lowland grasslands rather than the drier, densely canopied areas, the barasinghas are easy prey for poachers who are after their striking antlers. "Barasingha" means "12-tined"; the main antler stem grows tall and straight before branching out in graceful, arching curves. Herds form when the rutting season begins, bringing stags and hinds together, and the mating is heralded by the bugling of eager males staking out individual territories.

Axis deer, or chital (overleaf), are found mainly in Kanha Park in central India. Their delicate, spotted pattern is characteristic of this earliest of deer species, which has survived for 13 million years and is a favorite in many zoos.

A trio of barasinghas (right) pause in a glade, their chestnut brown coats glistening in the sun. The older antlered male is alert, lifting his muzzle to scent danger and cocking his ears to signal his wariness to the others. When frightened, swamp deer emit a piercing bark or scream.

Axis deer proceed along a riverbank close to the dense vegetation in which they frequently shelter from the sun. Salt licks are often found beside streams, where the deer scrape the mineral free with their sharp incisors. Bucks and does mingle all year, so the mating season of this species has never been clearly defined. At times, however, bucks leave the herds to shed their antlers and grow another pair, and return to impress the waiting females with their majestic new racks.

While a female macaque (left) keeps watch, a juvenile monkey nibbles placidly on a leaf. Macaques are particularly fond of figs, and eat both the leaves and the juicy fruit, which grow in Corbett National Park.

Juveniles playfully groom their mother (right). Grooming is a vital part of macaque social behavior, and an indication of rank and dominance. Those on the same hierarchical level groom each other for equivalent lengths of time; subordinates groom superiors for longer periods.

Erstwhile Gods

For thousands of years Indian custom invested the rhesus macaque with divine status. Hanuman, the Hindu monkey god, presided over the art of magic and was credited with having mysterious restorative powers. Today, macaques like the one shown at right above frequently live on the grounds of Hindu temples, enjoying the beneficence of local villagers. Macaques in the wild, however, are threatened by the trapping of younger animals for sale as pets and for experimental use, and by the waning of ancient Hindu taboos against killing them.

In Bengal, in northeastern India, macaques are protected in forest reserves such as Corbett National Park, which attracts large populations of the monkeys. Water is abundant there during the rainy season, and when local streams dry up, the macaques congregate near the Ramganga River. The average group includes about 24 individuals of both sexes and varying ages led by one mature dominant male. Macaques are highly irascible, aggressive creatures; to avoid anarchy the leader jealously maintains his dominant status, using symbolic threat postures to intimidate intruders and disruptive insiders, but usually avoiding violent physical encounters.

Death Dance

One of nature's most dramatic confrontations is that of the mongoose and the Indian cobra, a ritualized, precisely choreographed battle to the death. The mongoose comes to the fray cloaked in its reputation as one of the most voracious of carnivores. It devours frogs, fish, crabs, insects, birds and small mammals—in short, anything that moves quickly enough to attract its attention but not fast enough to escape its lethal bite. Traveling alone or in small groups of four to 12, the mongoose adapts equally well to densely vegetated, hilly countryside or arid, open expanses of sandy soil—exploring rocky crevices and other natural hiding places for prey.

When the mongoose encounters a cobra, the two square off in an active battle that may last for over an hour. The mongoose begins the ritual of combat with a series of rapid jumps. Agile and alert, the mongoose outmaneuvers the more cautious reptile, dancing around it, feigning attack and then retreating. As the snake approaches warily, the upper part of its body poised high above the ground, the mongoose flattens itself, stretching out to its full length, and then suddenly compresses its body and withdraws, confusing the snake. During the combat the cobra frequently bends low, attempting to strike, but the mongoose reacts with stunning speed, finally leaping and grasping the cobra on the back of the neck with its sharp teeth and cracking its skull.

A mongoose leaves its burrow (opposite) to embark on a day's hunt. Rather than taking its prey by surprise, the mongoose pursues its quarry with powerful, running leaps and makes the final kill with a lethal bite on the victim's neck.

In combat with a cobra (top), a mongoose lies flat on the ground as the snake approaches. The cobra poises to strike (bottom), its hood spread. But this is the mongoose's opportunity, since the cobra cannot defend itself well in this position.

Well fed, a recumbent tiger (left) enjoys a respite after the rigors of the hunt. A universal symbol of fearlessness and controlled power, this cat is adapted for stalking prey, not for running it down. A loner, it generally hunts and feeds on its own.

Lion cubs pad along a reserve trail (right). Already highly efficient hunting machines, they will eventually group together in prides of up to 30 individuals, sharing the responsibility for the kill and feeding together.

Restoring the Balance

The imposing Asian cats, the magnificent lions and Bengal tigers that once freely roamed the subcontinent, still conjure up an aura of adventure—the era of the British Empire in 19th century India, when English officers and maharajas hunted tigers from the backs of elephants. Such hunts took their toll, and the number of Indian tigers has dwindled from 40,000 at the turn of the century to around 3,000 today. Under "Project Tiger," started in 1973, nine large reserves were set aside, including one at Corbett National Park in the foothills of the Himalayas. In this grassy valley surrounded by forests, villagers and cattle were relocated and the natural habitat gradually restored by a state government sympathetic to wildlife management. Kanha Park in central India is another noteworthy reserve where the solitary great cats may stalk unmolested.

Some 200 Asiatic lions roam the forested regions of Gir Sanctuary in western India, descendants of the beasts that once ranged from Greece to eastern India. The grassland areas had been overgrazed by the domestic cattle of the Maldhari herdsmen, which caused a drop in the wildlife population, particularly the antelope and deer that were the lion's principal prey. When the lions turned their attention to livestock, a program to resettle the cattle was undertaken, and a wall was built around the sanctuary to restrict grazing animals. The stock of wild prey increased and ecological balance was restored.

A lesser panda, aroused from midday torpor, looks for the source of the disturbance (right). Generally nocturnal, it ordinarily prefers to sleep during the day, curling up in a leafy tree niche, tail over its head, or with its head tucked below its chest. The panda below displays the species' winsome facial expression. Pandas are usually gentle, but when they become frightened or disturbed, they may utter short whistles or squeaks while raising themselves on their hind legs in an unconvincing display of aggressiveness.

Panda Shangri-la

A more remote, inaccessible habitat than that of the Indian lesser panda would be difficult to imagine. The lesser panda rivals its raccoon relatives in appeal, with dark eye patches that give the "masked bandit" look characteristic of the species. It lives in the bamboo forests on the south-eastern slopes of the Himalayas—6,500 to 12,000 feet above sea level. The panda's high-altitude home is often foggy and cold, and always rugged. But the compact, sturdy panda has a rich, silky coat to serve as insulation; sharp, tapered claws to facilitate tree climbing; and thick, coarse hair on the soles of its feet to provide traction on slippery rocks, ice and snow. The lesser panda is primarily a ground feeder, nibbling on bamboo shoots and other vegetation of the region. Above all, because of the forbidding, isolated nature of its habitat, the lesser panda avoids many of the conflicts between man and animal that afflict wildlife elsewhere on the subcontinent.

Credits

Cover—G. Holton, Photo Researchers, Inc. 1–5—George Silk. 6–7—Y. Okamoto, Rapho Div., P.R., Inc. 9—Entheos. 17—K.W. Fink, Bruce Coleman, Inc. 18—E. Ricciati, P.R., Inc. 18–19 (bottom)—T. McHugh, P.R., Inc. 20–21—T. McHugh, P.R., Inc. 22–23—R. Kinne, P.R., Inc. 24–26—P. Coffey, Jersey Wildlife Preservation Trust. 28–29—Gail Rubin, B.C., Inc. 30–31—Peter B. Kaplan. 32–33—J.& D. Bartlett, B.C., Inc. 33—Peter B. Kaplan. 34 (top)—A. Mercieca, P.R., Inc. 34–35 (bottom)—K.W. Fink, B.C., Inc. 35—M. Heron, Woodfin Camp. 36–37—L. Stewart, *Sports Illustrated*, Time Inc. 37–39—M. Heron, Woodfin Camp. 41–42—Entheos. 43—Jim Brandenburg. 44–47—Entheos. 48–49—Jim Brandenburg. 49—Entheos. 50—Jim Brandenburg. 51 (top)—S. Grossman, Woodfin Camp; (bottom) D. DeVries, B.C., Inc. 52–55—Jim Brandenburg. 58—Entheos. 59–61—Jim Brandenburg. 63–65—J. & D. Bartlett, B.C., Inc. 66–67—C. Frank, P.R., Inc. 69—J. & C. Munoz, P.R., Inc. 70–71—J. & D. Bartlett, B.C., Inc. 72—F. Erize, B.C., Inc. 73— J. McDonald, B.C., Inc. 74–75—J. & D. Bartlett, B.C., Inc. 77—E. Duscher, B.C., Inc. 78 (top)—G. Plage, B.C., Inc.; (bottom) E. Duscher, B.C., Inc. 78–79—P. Jackson, B.C., Inc. 80 (top)—E. Duscher, B.C., Inc.; (bottom) E. Hosking, B.C., Inc. 81—S. Halvorsen, B.C., Inc. 82–83—J. Fernandez, B.C., Inc. 84–87—H. Silvestre, Rapho, P.R., Inc. 93–97—George Silk. 98 (top)—Oxford Scientific Films; (bottom) George Silk. 98–99—George Silk. 104—C. Haagner, B.C., Inc. 104–105—George Silk. 106–109—George Silk. 110–111—R. Kinne, P.R., Inc. 112–113—George Silk. 114—T. McHugh, P.R., Inc. 114–115—K. Tanaka, Animals Animals. 116–117—George Silk. 118—K. Tanaka, Animals Animals. 119—S. Nagendra, P.R., Inc. 120—E. Hanuman Rao, P.R., Inc. 121—P. Koch, P.R., Inc. 122—S. Wayman, P.R., Inc. 122–123— E.H. Rao, P.R., Inc. 124–125—G. Holton, P.R., Inc.

Photographs on endpapers are used courtesy of Time-Life Picture Agency, Russ Kinne and Stephen Dalton of Photo Researchers, Inc. and Nina Leen.

Film sequence on page 8 is from "Tigers of Kanha," a program in the Time-Life Television series *Wild, Wild World of Animals*.

ILLUSTRATIONS on page 11 and 14 courtesy of The Bettmann Archive. The illustration on page 12 is used by permission of Ringling Bros., Barnum and Bailey Circus, Harry Harding Collection. The illustration on page 15 courtesy of The National Gallery, London. Illustrations on pages 56–57 are by Chas. B. Slackman, those on pages 101–104 by John Groth.

Bibliography

Allen, Thomas R., *Vanishing Wildlife of North America*. National Geographic Society, 1974.

"The American Buffalo," Conservation Note 12. U.S. Department of the Interior/Fish and Wildlife Service. U.S. Government Printing Office, 1971.

Austin, Oliver L., Jr., and Arthur Singer, *Birds of the World*. Golden Press, 1961.

"Badlands National Monument South Dakota," U.S. Department of the Interior/ National Park Service. U.S. Government Printing Office, 1975.

Barnum, Phineas Taylor, *Barnum's Own Story*. Dover Publications, 1961.

Campbell, Sheldon, "Noah's Ark in tomorrow's zoo; animals are a-comin', two by two." *Smithsonian*, 8, March 1978, pp. 42–51.

Caras, Roger A., *North American Mammals: Fur-Bearing Animals of the United States and Canada*. Meredith Press, 1967.

Clark, Champ and the Editors of Time-Life Books, *The Badlands*. Time-Life Books, 1974.

Crowe, Philip Kingsland, *The Empty Ark*. Charles Scribner's Sons, 1967.

Curry-Lindahl, Kai, *Europe: A Natural History*. Random House, 1964.

——, *Let Them Live*. Morrow, 1972.

——, and Jean-Paul Harroy, *National Parks of the World*. Golden Press, 1972.

Darwin, Charles, *The Voyage of the Beagle*. J.M. Dent, 1945.

Davenport, William, "France's Wild, Watery South." *National Geographic*, Vol. 143, No. 5, May 1973, pp. 696–726.

De Shauensee, Rodolphe Meyer, *A Guide to the Birds of South America*. Livingston Publishing Co., 1970.

Fernandez, Juan Antonio, *Doñana: Spain's Wildlife Wilderness*. Taplinger, 1975.

Fisher, James, *Zoos of the World: The Story of Animals in Captivity*. Doubleday, 1967.

Gooders, John, *The Great Book of Birds*. The Dial Press, 1975.

Grzimek, Bernhard, *Grzimek's Animal Life Encyclopedia*. Van Nostrand Reinhold, 1975.

Hahn, Emily, *Animal Gardens*. Doubleday, 1967.

Huxley, Sir Julian, "The Coto Doñana," *Essays of a Humanist*. Harper and Row, 1964.

Larousse Encyclopedia of the Animal World. Larousse, 1975.

Livingston, Bernard, *Zoo: Animals, People, Places*. Arbor House, 1974.

"Pronghorn Antelope," Conservation Note 11.

U.S. Department of the Interior/Fish and Wildlife Service. U.S. Government Printing Office, 1966.

The Rand McNally Atlas of World Wildlife. Rand McNally and Company in association with Mitchell Beazley Ltd., 1973.

Ripley, S. Dillon, "Ecologist Returns to South Asia for Another Look." *Smithsonian*, 7, October 1976, pp. 104–113.

Ross-Macdonald, Malcolm, ed., *The World Wildlife Guide*. Viking Press, 1971.

Schaller, George, *The Deer and the Tiger*. University of Chicago Press, 1967.

Silvester, Hans, *Horses of the Camargue*. Viking Press, 1976.

Simpson, George Gaylord, *Attending Marvels*. Time-Life Books, 1965.

Singh, Arjan, *Tiger Haven*. Harper & Row, 1973.

Street, Philip, *Vanishing Animals: Preserving Nature's Rarities*. E.P. Dutton & Co., Inc., 1963.

"Theodore Roosevelt National Memorial Park North Dakota," U.S. Department of the Interior/National Park Service. U.S. Government Printing Office, 1975.

Tilden, Freeman, *The National Parks*. Knopf, 1970.

Walker, Ernest P., *Mammals of the World*. Johns Hopkins University Press, 1975.

Index

Aardwolf, 18
Addax, 28, 29
Africa, southern, 92–107
Alligator, 10
Antelope, 10, 16, 92, 94, 96–103, 108, 123
Ape, 16
Aristotle, 10
Arizona-Sonora Desert Museum, 8, 32
Armadillo, 62
Ass, wild, 28, 29, 108
Axis deer, 108, 115, 116
Aye-aye lemur, 8

Badger, 40, 50, 51, 76, 89
Badlands National Monument, 13, 40, 54–55, 59
Bailey, J. A., 12, 13
Barasingha, 114–115
Barcelona Zoo (Spain), 21
Barnum, P. T., 12, 13, 14
Basel Zoo (Switzerland), 22–23
Bat, 16
Beagle, H.M.S., 62
Bear, 12; polar, 23
Bengal tiger, 123
Bharaptpur Bird Sanctuary (India), 108
Bison, 13, 14, 40, 59; European, 14; Indian, 108; woods, 14
Black buck, 108
Black kite, 80, 81
Black-maned lion, 92, 94
Boa constrictor, 16
Boar, wild, 76, 89, 108
Bobcat, 40
Bontebok, 14
Bowery Menagerie (New York), 10
Bronx Zoo (New York), 7, 31
Brown-hooded gull, 71
Buck, black, 108
Buffalo, 108; water, 108
Bull snake, 40
Burrowing owl, 40
Bushmen, 100–103. *See also* San
Buteo erythronotus, 68
Buzzard, 80, 92; white-breasted, 68

Cacomistle. *See* Ringtail
Camargue, 76, 84–91
Camel, 16
Cape mountain zebra, 14
Cattle, 10, 14, 50, 92, 108, 123
Cavy: desert, 72, 73; Patagonian, 62, 72, 73, 74
Cheetah, 16, 36, 37, 92, 94, 95, 108
Chimpanzee, 16

"Chulu bear." *See* Coatimundi
Circuses, wild animals and, 12–13
Coatimundi, 32, 33
Cobra, 108, 120, 121
Columbus, Ohio, zoo, 22
Corbett National Park (India), 113, 118, 119, 123
Coto Doñana, 76, 78, 80–83
Cottontail rabbit, 40, 50, 53
Cougar, 62
Coyote, 8, 40, 49
Crab, 120
Crane, 16; Siberian white, 108
Crocodile, 108

Darwin, Charles, 62
Darwin's rhea, 62, 64, 65, 68
Deer, 10, 40, 62, 76, 82, 108, 123; axis, 108, 115, 116; fallow, 29, 76; hog, 108; mule, 54, 55; red, 76; swamp, 115; white-tailed, 55
Deer mouse, 40
Desert cavy, 72, 73
Dog, 13
Dolichotis, 67, 68
Dotterel, 64, 65
Duck, 76
Durrell, Gerald, 24

Eagle, 40; imperial, 76, 78, 80, 81, 83
Eland, 92, 100–103
Elephant, 10, 11, 12, 13, 14, 16, 92, 108, 123
Elephant seal, 62
Elk, 40
Endangered species, 8, 14, 16, 22, 24, 28, 34, 92, 108
Etosha Pan National Park (Namibia), 92
Etruscan shrew, 76
European bison, 14
European hare, 88, 89
Extinction, 8, 14, 29, 34, 36, 59, 62, 80

Fallow deer, 29, 76
Ferret, 40, 50, 51
Flamingo, 16, 76, 81, 106
Fox, 40, 76, 89; Patagonian gray, 70, 71
Frankfurt Zoo (West Germany), 18–19
Frog, 70, 120

Gallinule, purple, 76
Gazelle, 16
Gemsbok, 92, 96, 98
Gharial, 112, 113
Gir Forest (India), 14
Gir Sanctuary (India), 123

Giraffe, 10, 36, 37, 92
Goat, wild, 108
Goose, greylag, 76
Gopher, 50; pocket, 40
Gorilla, 8, 20, 21, 22, 35
Gray fox, Patagonian, 70, 71
Great Plains (U. S.), 40
Grevenbroek, Mike van, 29
Grey heron, 79
Greyhound, 10
Greylag goose, 76
Griffon vulture, 80
Ground sloth, Patagonian, 62
Ground squirrel, 50, 53
Grzimek, Bernhard, 8, 19
Guanaco, 62
Gull, 76; brown-hooded, 71

Hagenbeck, Carl, 16
Hai Bar South (Israel), 28–29
Hare, 76; European, 88, 89
Hartebeest, 99
Hartmann's mountain zebra, 92
Hatshepsut, Queen (Egypt), 10
Hawk, 40
Hedgehog, 76, 88, 89
Henry III, King (England), 11
Heron, 76, 78, 80, 81; grey, 79; purple, 90, 91; squacco, 78
Hog, pygmy, 108
Hog deer, 108
Horse, 13, 50; Przewalski's, 34, 35; wild, 16, 35, 76, 84–87
Huanaco, 67
Hudson, W. H., 67
Huemul, 62
Hyena, 92

Ibex, 16, 29, 76
Impala, 92
Imperial eagle, 76, 78, 80, 81, 83
India, 108–125
Indian bison, 108
Indian rhinoceros, 7, 22, 108, 110, 111

Jackal, 92, 108
Jackrabbit, 40
Jaguar, 12
Jersey Wildlife Preservation Trust, 24

Kalahari Gemsbok National Park (Botswana), 92, 94–103
Kanha National Park (India), 108, 115, 123
Kaziranga National Park (India), 108, 110–111, 115

King penguin, 22, 23
Kite, 78; black, 80, 81
Knoxville, Tennessee, zoo, 16
Kudu, 92; lesser, 96, 97

Lang, Ernst, 22
Lapwing, southern, 64, 65
Lemur, aye-aye, 8
Leopard, 10, 12, 92
Leopard cat, 30, 31
Lincoln, Abraham, 13
Lion, 10, 11, 12, 14, 16, 92, 122, 123;
    black-maned, 92, 94
Livingstone, David, 92
Lizard, 49, 62, 70
Llama, 16
London Zoo, 14, 16
Long-eared owl, 90, 91
Longhi, Pietro, painting by, 14
Loris, 30, 31
Louis XIV, King (France), 11
Louis XVI, King (France), 12
Lynx, 76, 82, 83; pardel, 76, 83

Macaque, 118, 119
Magpie, 78
Mara. See Cavy, Patagonian
Marmot, 50
Marten, 76
Martin, J., 10
Meerkat, 18, 104–105
Mongoose, 10, 76, 108, 120, 121
Monkey, 10, 14, 108; spider, 8
Mountain zebra: Cape, 14; Hartmann's, 92
Mouse, deer, 40
Muir, John, 13
Mule deer, 54, 55
Musk oxen, 23, 108

National Bison Range (Montana), 59
National parks, 8, 13–14, 59, 62, 92, 108,
    113, 118, 119, 123
National Zoo (Washington, D. C.), 7

Okapi, 19, 34, 35
Onager, 29
Opossum, 62
Orangutan, 19
Oryx, 29
Ostrich, 29
Owl, 10, 16; burrowing, 40; long-eared, 90,
    91

Panda, lesser, 124
Pardel lynx, 76, 83
Parks, national, 8, 13–14, 59, 62, 92, 108,
    113, 118, 119, 123
Partridge, 82
Patagonia, 62–75
Patagonian cavy, 62, 72, 73, 74
Patagonian gray fox, 70, 71
Patagonian ground sloth, 62
Penguin, 16, 62, 73, 74; king, 22,
    23
Piranha, 10
Pliny the Elder, 11
Plover, 64
Pocket gopher, 40
Polar bear, 23
Polecat, 76
Porcupine, 94
Post, Laurens van der, 100
Prairie dog, 40, 42–47, 49, 50, 51
Pratincole, 78
Preserves, 8, 14, 16, 19, 40, 76, 92, 108,
    115
Pronghorn, 40
Przewalski's horse, 34, 35
Pudu, 62
Puma, 67
Purple gallinule, 76
Purple heron, 90, 91
Pygmy hog, 108
Python, 108

Rabbit, 10, 40, 49, 62, 70, 82; Assam, 108;
    cottontail, 40, 50, 53; jack, 40
Rat, 10
Rattlesnake, 40
Red deer, 76
Reserves, 8, 14, 59, 92, 96, 123
Rhea, 62; Darwin's, 62, 64, 65, 68
Rhinoceros, 14, 36; Indian, 7, 22, 108, 110,
    111; white, 14, 36, 37
Right whale, 62
Rinderpest, 92
Ringling, Charles, 13
Ringling Bros., Barnum & Bailey Circus,
    12–13
Ringtail, 32, 33
Roosevelt, Theodore, 13

San, 92, 100. See also Bushmen
San Diego Zoo, 16, 34–39
Scorpion, 104

Sea lion, 62
Seal, 13; elephant, 62
Serengeti National Park, 19
Sheep, 10, 70; wild, 16, 76, 108
Shrew, 76; Etruscan, 76
Siberian white crane, 108
Sloth, Patagonian ground, 62
Spider monkey, 8
Spoonbill, 78, 79
Springbok, 92, 98
Squacco heron, 78
Squirrel, ground, 50, 53
Steenbok, 92, 96, 97
Stevenson-Hamilton, J., 13
Stork, 78, 83
Suricate. See Meerkat
Swamp deer, 115

Tapir, 24–27
Tern, 76
Theodore Roosevelt National Memorial
    Park (North Dakota), 40
Tiger, 10, 12, 108; Bengal, 123
Tinamou, 68
Tragopan, 108

Varro, 11
Vulture, 80, 92; griffon, 80

Water buffalo, 108
Weasel, 76
Wen Wang, Emperor (China), 10
Whale, right, 62
White-breasted buzzard, 68
White crane, Siberian, 108
White rhinoceros, 14, 36, 37
White-tailed deer, 55
Wild Animal Park (San Diego Zoo), 34,
    36–37
Wildcat, 10, 76
Wildebeest, 14, 92
Wind Cave National Park (South Dakota),
    59
Wolf, maned, 19
Woods bison, 14
World Wildlife Fund, 76

Yellowstone National Park, 13, 59
Yosemite Valley, 13

Zebra, 16, 92; Cape mountain, 14;
    Hartmann's mountain, 92
Zoos, 8, 16–39